GOD'S HERE AND NOW

EXPLORING FAITH

Theology for Life

SERIES EDITORS: Leslie J Francis and Jeff Astley

GOD'S HERE AND NOW

Social Contexts of the Ministry of the People of God

Philip Richter

with

John Eade
Stuart Jordan
Robert Moore
Anthony Russell
Mark Wakelin

DARTON · LONGMAN + TODD

First published in 1999 by
Darton, Longman and Todd Ltd
1 Spencer Court
140-142 Wandsworth High Street
London SW18 4JJ

ISBN 0-232-52346-0

A catalogue record for this book is available from the British Library.

Designed by Sandie Boccacci
Phototypeset in Minion by Intype London Ltd
Printed and bound in Great Britain by
Page Bros, Norwich, Norfolk

CONTENTS

CONTRIBUTORS

Dr John Eade, Principal Lecturer in Sociology and Social Policy, Roehampton Institute, London.

The Revd Dr Stuart Jordan, Secretary, The Methodist Church London Committee.

Professor Robert Moore, Eleanor Rathbone Professor of Sociology, University of Liverpool.

The Revd Philip Richter, Educational Development Officer, The Southern Theological Education and Training Scheme.

The Rt Revd Anthony Russell, Bishop of Dorchester.

The Revd Mark Wakelin, Methodist Association of Youth Clubs National Secretary and suburban ministry practitioner.

ACKNOWLEDGEMENTS

Chapters 1 and 2 were based on material by John Eade. Chapters 3 and 4 were based on material by Robert Moore. Chapters 5 and 6 were written by Stuart Jordan based on material by Linda Pickens-Jones and Alan Jones. Chapters 7 and 8 were based on material by Mark Wakelin. Chapters 9 and 10 were based on material by Anthony Russell.

PREFACE

At the beginning of the third millennium a new mood is sweeping through the Christian churches. This mood is reflected in a more radical commitment to discipleship among a laity who wish to be theologically informed and fully equipped for Christian ministry in the secular world.

Exploring Faith: theology for life is designed for people who want to take Christian theology seriously. Taken seriously, Christian theology engages the mind, involves the heart, and seeks active expression in the way we live. Those who explore their faith in this way are beginning to shape a theology for life.

Exploring Faith: theology for life is rooted in the individual experience of the world and in the ways through which God is made known in the world. Such experience is related to and interpreted in the light of the Christian tradition. Each volume in the series takes a key aspect of theology, and explores this aspect in dialogue with the readers' own experience. Each volume is written by a scholar who has clear authority in the area of theology discussed and who takes seriously the ways in which busy adults learn.

The volumes are suitable for all those who wish to learn more about the Christian faith and ministry, including those who have already taken Christian basic courses (such as *Alpha* and *Emmaus*) and have been inspired to undertake further study, those preparing to take theology as an undergraduate course, and those already engaged on degree programmes. The volumes have been developed for individuals to work on alone or for groups to study together.

Already groups of Christians are using the *Exploring Faith: theology for life* series throughout the United Kingdom, linked by an exciting initiative pioneered jointly by the Anglican dioceses, the Board of Education of the Church and World Division and the Ministry Division of the Archbishops' Council of the Church of England, the National Society and the Church Colleges. Used in this way each volume can earn credits towards one of the Church Colleges' Certificates and provide access to degree level study. Further information about the Church Colleges' Certificate Programme is provided on page 126.

The Church Colleges' Certificate Programme integrates well with the lifelong learning agenda which now plays such a crucial role in educational priorities. Learning Christians can find their way into degree-bearing programmes through this series *Exploring Faith: theology for life* linked with the Church Colleges Certificates.

In preparing a series of this kind, much work is done behind the scenes. Financial and staff support have been generously given by the Ministry Division. Thanks are due to Marilyn Parry for the vision of bringing together the Aston materials and the Anglican Church Colleges of Higher Education. Thanks also should go to the Aston staff and the original authors for being willing to make the materials available for reworking. We are also grateful for financial support from the following Church Colleges: Chester College; Christ Church University College, Canterbury; The College of St Mark and St John, Plymouth; St Martin's College, Lancaster; Trinity College Carmarthen; and Whitelands College (Roehampton Institute). Without the industry, patience, perception, commitment and skill of Ruth Ackroyd this series would have remained but a dream.

The series editors wish to express their personal thanks to colleagues who have helped them shape the series identity, especially Diane Drayson, Ros Fane, Evelyn Jackson, Anne Rees and Morag Reeve, and to the individual authors who have produced high-quality text on schedule and so generously accepted firm editorial direction. The editorial work has been supported by the North of England Institute for Christian Education and the Centre for Theology and Education at Trinity College Carmarthen.

Leslie J Francis
Jeff Astley

INTRODUCTION

The human person is inevitably part and parcel of a particular society, and it is within the fabric of that society that God's Kingdom is experienced, discerned and expressed. In this book we invite you to take a careful look at a range of different social contexts in Britain today, including your own. Every social context is unique, but also displays characteristics common to other similar contexts. Our aim is to help you to become more aware of some of these common features, so that the people of God can best be enabled to engage with God's here and now.

This book focuses on five contexts for the ministry of the people of God: global, communal, urban, suburban and rural. You will find that there is some overlap between these contexts, not least because the last three contexts for ministry will be largely defined in terms of geographical location, whilst the first two contexts are more broadly conceived.

We begin by exploring what it means to live in a 'global village'. Technological innovations and economic changes have propelled our society into a new 'globalised' context. Global capitalism impinges directly on people's everyday lives. But globalisation is not just an economic process: it has important social and cultural effects. Networking is now possible on a global scale. There is currently a fascinating interplay between global and local processes. On the one hand, there is the danger that globalisation may entail greater standardisation, homogeneity and centralised control. On the other hand it has also encouraged diversity and launched new methods of communication media capable, for example, of supporting local struggles against global sources of injustice.

We move on to examine the communal context for ministry. We consider whether community is simply a 'village in the mind' or whether there are real social formations that we can identify as communities. Communities are typically conceived in geographic and economic terms. We highlight the dangers of romanticising bygone rural communities. We also consider communities of interest, including ethnic and virtual cyber communities. Our analysis challenges churches to recognise that talk of 'community' may sometimes be an excuse for fuzzy thinking, concealing and reinforcing conflicts of interests and power inequalities.

Next we analyse urban contexts for ministry. Churches have often found it difficult to adapt to the realities of urban life and have tended to picture the city in negative terms. We explore an approach to Christian urban theology that can enable the church to approach the urban context with a different attitude and means of analysis, based in a dynamic interaction of biblical, social, political and economic analysis. This approach celebrates the city as a key place of God's self-disclosure and reconceptualises the city as 'God's sacred place'.

We move on to explore suburban contexts for ministry. Suburbia is preoccupied with questions of neighbourhood, community and identity; this reflects profound uncertainties within suburbia about these issues. Although suburbia sometimes appears static, complacent and detached, underneath the surface it is a community on the move, inherently discontented and externally dependent. While it is not the case that suburbia is profoundly religious, its inherent discontent and longing for the new may help prepare people for the possibility of a spiritual journey. Churches must beware, however, of confusing the suburban agenda and the gospel agenda. The key themes of the gospel message both resonate with and disturb suburban churches.

Finally, we examine rural contexts for ministry. There has been increasing population movement into the countryside on the part of commuters, second-home owners and retired people. This has accentuated some of the social and economic divisions in rural areas. Our analysis discloses that the 'village community' is actually the product of interaction between three disparate communities: the farming community, the old village community and the new village community. We challenge presuppositions of 'rural idylls' and highlight the countryside as a place of contrasts, characterised by both affluence and deprivation. Unlike in many urban areas, the church seldom has to fight its way into the rural community: the church still has an acknowledged part to play in this particular social context.

1. THE WORLD ON THE DOORSTEP

Introduction

In this chapter we shall:
- explore what it means to live in a 'global village';
- analyse the impact of globalisation on the economy;
- discuss some of the effects of the communications revolution.

  In chapters 1 and 2 you are invited to imagine that you are reading two letters from a (Roman Catholic) sociologist to his parish priest.

> **Reflecting on experience**
> Where did the ingredients for your main meal today come from? Are they mainly local in origin or do they mostly come from other parts of the globe? Do you make a conscious effort to buy locally produced products or does it not matter?

Locality

Dear Michael,

  I have just got back from a trip to the USA, hence the long delay in replying to your invitation to dinner. Yes, we'd love to come but be warned – we might bore everyone with our travellers' tales!

  I know you are interested in matters beyond our parish, given your missionary experience in rural Zambia and your frequent return visits to Zambia and other African countries. In our many discussions I have argued that there are numerous ways in which our local communities are affected by outside events and I know that I have talked for far too long sometimes about the dreaded 'g' word – globalisation. Anyway, bear with me once more as I return to the theme in the context of my American visit.

First let me remind you about the debates concerning the intense attachments which people have towards their local community. You talk about it a good deal in your provocative sermons, and the whole concept of a congregation attached to a particular church or chapel inevitably celebrates locality. People walk to their place of worship or drive short distances on a quiet Sunday morning. They see neighbours and make friendships with others who live nearby, or at least within easy visiting distance.

Furthermore, we are encouraged in gospel readings to have a Christian concern for our neighbour, and in our prayers we remember the joys and sorrows of loved ones. We go to funerals or weddings where there is usually some local connection, however tenuous! The wedding reception or the post-funeral tea is held in a local hall, hotel, restaurant or family home. Speeches are made at the wedding reception about the lives of the bride and groom which frequently focus on their escapades and foibles as members of the local family home. Frequently the subdued chat over the tea and sandwiches after a funeral centres on the contribution made by the deceased person to his or her family and local community. Photographs, memories and periodical visits to the church or chapel maintain the link with the local community. Those flowers by the graveside are a mute testimony to those continuing associations with a particular place. Of course, as you often remind me, they are much more than that, but I am not trying to tell the whole story here!

EXERCISE

📖 **Read John 3:16–17.** Although the church is called to embody the gospel locally, the gospel is never simply for one time or place.

How effectively does your church communicate the fact that it stands for global salvation?

Anyway, what has all this to do with my recent trip, I hear you saying?! Well, what struck me initially was how intense were the attachments of my American friends to their own locality. At the airport a large billboard welcomed me to the local municipal area of Wilmington. I hired a car whose number plate proclaimed the wider territory in which this locality was administratively and politically contained – 'North Carolina: First in Flight'. (The American desire to be first extends to its states evidently. I learned later that 'First in Flight' refers to the Wright Brothers' pioneering glide over the coastal sand dunes in 1903. Does this historical nugget stir distant childhood memories of famous human achievements?)

As I drove into Wilmington I was introduced to the localities within the Wilmington municipality as the suburban sprawl of urban America welcomed us to Ogden, Carolina Beach, Wrightsville, Moore's Creek, and directed visitors to its older core, 'historic downtown Wilmington'. Once I had recovered from jet lag (far worse after the return flight I might add!) I combined business with pleasure in a very agreeable way – meeting people at the university where I was making an exchange and dining in their homes, shopping in the suburban malls, walking round the downtown area and eating wonderful cookies and cheesecakes in one particular restaurant, watching loads of television channels in a desperate bid to find one which did not have adverts every five minutes. On Sunday I attended a local church which was packed to the rafters by a congregation engaged in a busy schedule of weekly good works and community activities.

From these, and a wealth of passing encounters within Wilmington and further afield, I became aware of a deep pride in different localities. Yet here we come to the nub of my argument about the 'wider world'. This pride was shaped by wider loyalties. What appeared at first sight to be a rock solid, unchanging, highly traditional corner of America was revealed under closer inspection to be a less stable, more dynamic and varied society where the past was continually being reinterpreted in the light of present developments, and where people were continually speculating about what the future might bring.

The wider world

As I have already mentioned, the sense of belonging to a wider world is proclaimed on every local car number plate which celebrates the state of North Carolina. An even wider, national allegiance is affirmed by the Stars and Stripes flown from flag poles on houses and in their gardens, shopping malls, public buildings and displayed on jeans, T-shirts and trainers. In this area of the United States, which fought on the side of the Confederacy during the American Civil War and which played its part as the 'last major stronghold of the Confederacy', another flag is frequently to be seen reminding people of the traditions of the 'South'. The 'South' conjures up images of plantations and languid southern belles (*Gone with the Wind* and all that) but it also raises the issues of slavery, racial discrimination and segregation. My drive en route to 'historic downtown Wilmington' through the rundown area inhabited totally (as far as I could see) by African Americans indicates that these issues are not just 'history' for local people.

So clearly Wilmingtonians are linked by history and by contemporary economic and political institutions to a wider America and to America's social tensions and conflicts. I hear you saying: 'So what! Tell us something new.' All right, then, let's take the exploration of this wider world further. There is no reason why we should stop at the national frontier despite the profound patriotism of many Americans and their pre-occupation with events in their own country. I am sometimes reminded of the heyday of British imperial superiority which was captured in the celebrated newspaper hoarding proclaiming: 'Storms in the Channel: Continent isolated'!

In my opinion Americans are far less insular than they were. The emergence of serious economic competition from Western Europe and now the Pacific Rim countries (Japan, Taiwan and South Korea in particular) has made them highly conscious of the impact of such competition on their own economy. The symbol of the American good life, the car, provides a good illustration of what has been happening. When I arrived I promptly hired a car from Hertz who provided me – guess what? – with a neat, economical Japanese car. As I drove into Wilmington the car found itself surrounded by its Asian cousins.

When I entered the motel room I switched on a Japanese-licensed television set which showed adverts encouraging the viewer to buy Pacific Rim products. The local supermarket stocked not only American farm goods but also French wines, German beer and Mexican fruit. At a chain store near a seaside resort on the way to Charleston I was able to buy a colourful cotton shirt made in Bangladesh, and flirted with the idea of buying a pair of trainers marketed by a British company but made in the Philippines.

The American media has used the term 'globalisation' to describe this rapidly changing balance of economic power. President Clinton made considerable play of the threat from Pacific Rim imports when he was first elected. He also claimed that American students, the next generation of producers if you like, need to be taught a greater awareness of the world beyond their shores if the USA is to fight back against these developments in the global economy.

The international and global economy

What I have discussed so far may not appear to be so very new. After all, have we not in Britain been well aware for a long time that we are part of an international economy despite the tendency of 'little Englanders' to speak as though the storms in the Channel still raged, isolating us from not only the Continent but the wider world in general? However, what is new is that we live in a world where two economies co-exist, an international *and* a global economy. Trade and production is no longer principally based on national foundations and agreements between nations. The very large companies look beyond national boundaries to global links where national allegiances play a still important but diminished role. They are called *transnational* companies because they can operate across national frontiers and interests. The administrative headquarters of such a company may be in London, for example, but its centre of financial operations may be located in an off-shore tax haven (the Cayman Islands or the Bahamas) while its manufacturing base may be in a low-cost 'industrialising' country like Thailand, Malaysia or the Philippines. Those who work for the company can be moved around this transnational structure as can material resources, depending, of course, on changing local political conditions.

I am sorry if I have begun another lecture! My visit to the USA has made me think quite a lot about these developments as you can see. (You have commented on how you have become reflective yourself after returning from your visits to Anglican missions in Africa.) What concerns both of us from our different perspectives is the impact of these economic developments on people's everyday lives. How is globalisation actually experienced in the localities which we inhabit?

What we share with our American cousins is a growing realisation that the flexibility of global flows of capital means that nations can no longer control their own destinies. Perhaps I should rephrase that statement since such a state of affairs has existed for a very long time in Britain, whereas the USA is only just coming to terms with global interdependence. So let's put it this way: we live in an increasingly interdependent world where capital is organised on a transnational, global scale despite nationalist rhetorics about autonomy and independence. 'Buy British' was always a naïve slogan, but the possibility that production can be organised solely on a national scale has rapidly receded as the global economy has strengthened.

EXERCISE

How does the global mobility of capital affect social and economic conditions in the United Kingdom?

Has your working life, or that of your friends or family, ever been adversely affected by decisions to relocate production abroad?

Were these decisions taken in this country or another country?

To what extent did you feel that the decisions were taken on the grounds of expediency and cost?

To what extent did you feel that the decisions were in your short- or long-term interest?

How can the church best offer pastoral support at such a time?

The impact on everyday life is multi-faceted: it is not only economic but also political, social, cultural and environmental. (There are other areas of life – psychological, philosophical and theological, for example – but I am not equipped to pursue these in any depth.) We now think and talk about the world as a discrete entity. We worry about global warming, we read about trade agreements between members of the global economy (the GATT Talks and the Uruguay Round) and the dangers of excluding the 'Third World' and an even more impoverished 'Fourth World' from the wealth generated through global capitalism. We read about political violence associated with ethnic revivalism and religious 'fundamentalism', and we still dread the threat of nuclear holocaust. In our most immediate lives, we ponder the substantial numbers of permanently unemployed people in Britain and whether we can only compete on the global stage by becoming a low-cost, low-wage economy where a minute élite earn relatively enormous earnings.

So the people you encounter as a priest – the unemployed, those in a job but worried about losing it, the homeless, those trying to keep up with their rent and mortgage payments, their children at school and college wondering about their future, those facing environmental disaster in Africa or seeking treatment in your mission hospitals, your own family and relatives – are also grappling with forces which extend far beyond their localities and which are, to some extent, beyond their individual control. You do not have to be a Marxist to see that the operation of global capitalism has a profound effect on the way everyone on this planet conducts his or her individual life.

Global networking

Ironically, globalisation provides us with the capacity to co-operate in directing these forces the way we would like them to go. Our daily newspapers record the diverse ways in which we fail to achieve this cooperation but the media shows us also that collaboration on a global scale already takes place. We are increasingly aware of the possibilities (I put it no stronger than that) of widening and strengthening that collaboration.

EXERCISE

Would you welcome greater global collaboration?

Is it possible to achieve collaboration on this scale?

Might the world just disintegrate into so many nationalisms?

What specific issues and concerns, if any, might prompt countries to collaborate on a global scale?

How does globalisation provide us with this capacity, I hear you ask! One way is through the technological innovations which have produced a shrinking world. These innovations include the railway, steam- and then oil-powered ships, the aeroplane, the car, radio, television, camera, video, computer, telephone, telegraph, telegram, fax and electronic mail. Although some of these innovations are hardly new, the world has shrunk with greater and greater speed as technological products have become cheaper and more widely available. Anyone who lives in London knows from everyday experience how rapidly car ownership has increased in the capital over the last ten years! We are also beginning to take for granted certain relatively recent innovations such as the television, video recorder and camcorder, adding them to our list of 'indispensable' consumer goods such as the radio, camera, refrigerator and washing machine.

The effect of the innovations which enable us to communicate with one another (the airmail letter, telephone, camera photograph, video, television, fax and electronic mail) is to establish a world where contact can be relatively easily established with people across the globe. While connections could be maintained with family and friends across the world a hundred years ago, those links were slow, not very reliable or not widely used. Now I can pick up a phone and ring almost anyone aided and abetted by the telecommunications satellites out there in space. I know that only a small minority of people have access to a fax and even fewer use electronic mail, but these technological innovations make it so easy to maintain detailed and prolonged contact with people one may never have met in the flesh, as it were. Furthermore, these innovations, just like the radio, television and telephone twenty years ago, will become more widely available as people become more aware of them and their uses.

EXERCISE

📖 **Read the story of the Tower of Babel in Genesis 11:1–9.** This is a story about primeval time and tells of God's scattering of people over the face of the earth and the confusion of their languages. It may originally have been a story intended to explain why human beings speak different languages.

Globalisation seems to move in the opposite direction to this story, since it seems to draw people together in new ways through modern forms of global interdependence and communication.

Should the story of Babel be taken as a theological warning against globalisation? Why or why not?

The social and cultural consequence of these technological developments is to diminish the distances of time and space between us and our local lives. We can almost immediately send messages around the world and we can receive a reply just as quickly. Private space can become available to anyone who wants to get in touch with us, with terrifying or embarrassing consequences if we do not want others to know where we are! I know you hate mobile phones but at least they allow people to talk to each other even when they are walking along the street or driving their car. I agree that there should be some time and space in our lives when we are free from others, but we can get that by taking the phone off the hook, switching the mobile phone off or installing an answerphone!

So globalisation is not just an economic process: it has important social and cultural effects. It shapes our relations with other people across the world and it impacts on the way we perceive the world. We can establish and maintain relationships with people we might never or hardly ever meet, and the distances of space and time between us and them diminish on a scale never possible before.

The possibilities of networking on a global scale are vastly increased, therefore, as technological innovation proceeds. Global communication is not simply the preserve of world élites such as members of the various world organisations (the United Nations, the World Bank, the World Health Organisation, the International Monetary Fund), regional power blocs (such as the Pacific Rim countries, the USA and the European Union) and non-governmental organisations (such as Amnesty International, Greenpeace or the Friends of the Earth). Smaller, less powerful and far more local groups can make use of these technological innovations to resist the power of these more global organisations, to lobby them or to make alliances with them.

We have seen this most clearly during local campaigns over such issues as nuclear disarmament, whaling, road-building and environmental damage, or the torture of political prisoners. The Greenham Common women, Twyford Down and the Greenpeace ship have become symbols of resistance to the power of national and international interests which can be communicated across the world through television, radio, newspapers, film and books. Popular music can celebrate their struggles and satellites can disperse their message across the globe.

EXERCISE

What are your experiences of the World Wide Web? If a group of you are working together, exchange and discuss your experiences.

What do you see to be the benefits and dangers of the World Wide Web?

Reflecting on the World Wide Web

The globalised World Wide Web has become a powerful tool for protest groups. The Internet is a profoundly democratic medium of communication. Originally developed as a secure, nuclear-bomb-proof military communications network in the 1960s, by the mid 1990s it had evolved into the World Wide Web, allowing anyone with the requisite computer equipment instant access to information and e-mail communication worldwide. The World Wide Web is both a tool of the global economy, daily facilitating myriads of transnational electronic transactions, and also potentially a potent tool for those seeking to resist globalism and the rampant free market. It is a means of communication for global giants but, equally, also a means for local activists and pressure groups to disseminate information and to forge wider alliances.

The World Wide Web was arguably a crucial factor in the downfall of the proposed international Multilateral Agreement on Investment (MAI). The Agreement, which would have given enormous legal and economic advantages to transnational corporations at the expense of national jurisdictions and civil liberties, had originally been debated in secret by OECD countries. Once details had been leaked, the campaign against MAI spread like wildfire, thanks to the World Wide Web. Within two years, over 600 protest groups, in different countries, were exchanging information and effectively undermining the negotiating positions of individual governments.

Unlike the printed word, it is difficult to censor the Internet, although some governments have sought to control access. In Myanmar unauthorised online activity can attract a term of fifteen years' imprisonment. China does not allow its citizens access to the newsgroup area of the Internet, afraid, perhaps, that newsgroup discussions might promote too much freedom of speech.

Some have argued that freedom of expression on the Internet is not always desirable, even within Western democracies. In February 1999 anti-abortionists in Oregon were fined $107.9 million for allowing a list of 'wanted' abortion doctors to appear on their website. In this case considerations relating to the potential threat to the doctors' safety transcended those of freedom of speech.

Some censorship is desirable. Parents are right to be concerned about the risks to their children from violent or pornographic material on the Internet. They are wise to install software to filter out undesirable sites.

The Internet is by its very nature a difficult medium to police. For the time being, at least, and for the first time in human history, people can have access to a truly global and democratic means of communication.

Empowerment

'Surely,' you may now be saying, 'your experience and mine, both in this country and in Africa and India, shows how very few people can engage in this world of sophisticated technology. Our experience also tells us how much more powerful are global companies as well as international and national political élites at getting what they want. The African and Indian peasant is concerned about the next harvest and basic survival, not communicating with others around the world with sophisticated and expensive consumer goods. Even if certain organisations highlight the plight of peasant farmers in different parts of the world, they have not changed the gradual spread of environmental disaster in sub-Saharan Africa nor the economic decline of many Third and Fourth World countries. The spread of global communications has only increased the power of wealthy capitalist countries, and global capitalism largely serves the interests of highly developed, industrialised countries.'

I agree with a lot of the words which I have put into your own mouth! We are clearly looking at an unequal distribution of resources. The actors on the world stage are not equal by any means and I know that your sense of outrage at this inequality sustains your work with those who are victims of the powerful. However, I also share your belief that everyone is powerful in their own way: no one is without power, nobody is power*less*. My point is that the technological innovations which I have described are being used to represent the interests of those resisting the power of global corporations and national and international élites. Of course it is an unequal struggle, given the way resources are currently distributed; but at least the problems of local groups can reach the wider world, alliances can be established between different local groups; and global communications can be used to pressurise international, national and local policy-makers into changing their plans.

Best wishes,
John

EXERCISE

How does looking at things on a global scale affect your attitude to problems in this country?

In parts of Africa and in some other parts of the world, we are dealing with absolute poverty, whereas in the western world we are concerned with relative poverty. Some people, particularly in the churches, feel that we should concentrate on combating absolute poverty, rather than using our energy to deal with the less life-threatening poverty experienced here. How do you respond to that line of reasoning?

Further reading

Albrow, M and King, E (1990), *Globalization, Knowledge and Society*, London, Sage.

Eade, J (1997), *Living the Global City*, London, Routledge.

Featherstone, M (ed.) (1990), *Global Culture: nationalism, globalization and modernity*, London, Sage.

Giddens, A (1999), *Globalisation: Reith Lectures 1999* (forthcoming).

Robertson, R (1992), *Globalization*, London, Sage.

2. ONE WORLD OR MANY?

Introduction

In this chapter we shall:
- explore the interplay between global and local factors in today's world;
- identify tendencies towards both standardisation and diversity;
- discuss the relativising and universalising effects of globalisation.

In this chapter you are invited to imagine that you are reading the second letter from a (Roman Catholic) sociologist to his parish priest.

Reflecting on experience

How powerful do you think the United States is in the world? To what extent are you affected by American policies or military actions? What American products do you consume? How far are your values and beliefs shaped by watching American films and television programmes?

It has been suggested that American popular culture and foreign policy is dominated not by Christian love for the enemy but by the imperative to exterminate the enemy (Wink, 1992, p. 13); to what extent has this affected your attitude towards enemies?

Americanisation?

Dear Michael,

What we are looking at today, I believe, is a fascinating interplay between global and local processes. Our perceptions of local communities and their needs are shaped by global economic, political and social developments which operate across national boundaries and beyond agreements between nations. However, this is not a one-way process. Local organisations and individuals can use global communications to build alliances across different localities and pressurise those operating at more global levels and at the level of the global itself. Consequently, injustices can no longer be contained simply at the local or even the national level. Conflict in Bosnia, Kosovo, Somalia, Iraq and Northern Ireland are dealt with by international agencies on a long-established pattern of nation-state agreements. Yet, these conflicts escape the controls of these agencies since they are also shaped by the flow of information and images through the global media and by communities dispersed around the globe. Consider, for example, the use made by IRA leaders in Northern Ireland of the global media and the substantial support which they have received among Irish Americans.

As we have discussed on many occasions, these and other examples could easily be countered with the argument: 'All you are revealing is the power of the USA since it has played the key role on the international stage through the UN, IMF, NATO, and the World Bank. Without American military and financial support the UN and NATO would be toothless. These international bodies are really run by one particular nation, the superpower which is the USA.' Of course, the USA does play a major part in these regional conflicts but its power is limited by the need to work with others.

War has to be waged on both an international and global stage. During the Gulf War, the Bosnia crisis and, more recently, in Kosovo, American military might was crucially underpinned by a complex alliance where other nations' sensibilities had to be carefully considered. In the Gulf a major issue was the presence of American troops, especially women, in Saudi Arabia; while during the protracted struggle across the Balkans American strategy was influenced by the differing interests of national allies as well as the Serbian ally, Russia. These international alliances and enmities were, at the same time, expressed through the global media as images of destroyed bridges, burning oil wells, 'collateral damage' and fleeing refugees which affected popular opinion among countries around the world. A regional conflict involving different nation-states was acted out on the global stage through newspapers, radio and television.

If we get away from politics and war to life in our own neck of the woods, we can see that the development of global forces is not the same as Americanisation. Much has been made of the deepening influence of standardised American goods on other national ways of life. Critics have spoken of globalisation in terms of homogenisation and of the threat of American cultural and commercial hegemony. Commentators have pointed to the success which Coca-Cola and McDonald's have enjoyed in marketing and selling their products across the world. It is difficult to escape the Coca-Cola bottle or its copies wherever one goes as we know from our many cooling drinks in Cairo, Lusaka or Calcutta. You have often complained about young people's love of McDonald's burgers, processed french fries and apple pie: items which are recognisable in Warsaw, Manila, Rio de Janeiro and even the home of high-class cuisine, France, where there is a McDonald's in the Champs Elysees! One of the attractions of eating at McDonald's is that you can be certain of enjoying fundamentally the same product wherever you may happen to be in the world. The search for standard global products has widened with the production of the first global car by Ford, the Mondeo, which can be sold anywhere around the world with little or no concessions to regional or local tastes.

Standardisation on a global level is associated with American corporations but we have already seen that others now contribute to this process, and that Americanisation is only one form in which globalisation is expressed. The establishment of Japanese-run car assembly plants in Britain has had a dramatic impact on relations between management and organised labour in the car industry, for example. In the area of entertainment, while we receive game shows and films from the USA we also export our television plays, films and comedy programmes across the world. In my Wilmington motel room I could watch a whole channel devoted to British 'high-quality' shows including Patricia Routledge playing the redoubtable Mrs Bucket (pronounced 'Bouquet') in *Keeping Up Appearances*.

The World Wide Web has been perceived by some critics as a potent tool of American dominance. The Web originated in the United States. Up to 70 per cent of web communications are to or from North American sites. Companies in the United States do not need to use a national domain suffix for their website addresses: the Web is home territory. Since the origins of the Web lie in the English-speaking scientific community, some have also seen it as an example of the dominance of English as a world language. At the moment the Web is primarily a medium for the typed word. This empowers the literate and the technologically able but marginalises others. The Web tends to reinforce the dominance of the spoken and written (English) word in global culture. Any human experiences that cannot easily be communicated in words, such as religious experience, risk being marginalised. The Web is a prosaic medium that, paradoxically, may limit as well as expand people's horizons.

EXERCISE

How fair is the criticism of the World Wide Web as a potent tool of American dominance?

How far does the World Wide Web foster new inequalities across the world?

Homogenisation or diversity?

Globalisation certainly encourages standardisation, and Americanisation can be a particular but very widespread expression of that process, as virtually identical American products are exported all over the world. However, as I have already argued, globalisation can also enable local products, campaigns and alliances to find a wider audience. The purchase, for instance, of African and Indian 'ethnic' goods in London can encourage the production of those goods through the development of local traditional skills in rural areas. The massive increase in global travel and tourism as well as films about 'exotic' parts of the world are major factors in enabling those goods to reach a wider audience. It may appear paradoxical but greater diversity is actually enabled through global communications.

Diversity and fragmentation are also features of globalisation, making it possible for people to make their own personalised choices from the immense cornucopia of products, values and lifestyles on offer. British consumers have become infinitely more adventurous over what they will eat. Ethnic dishes, virtually unknown in Britain until the last three decades, have taken their place alongside traditional 'meat and two veg' cuisine. The popularity of television programmes dealing with home and garden improvement reflects individuals' desire to create a personalised living space that does not have to fit a standard mould, although it may contain design ingredients from many different global sources.

EXERCISE

What experiences have members of your local church had of living in other areas of Britain and in other parts of the world?

Do any members of your congregation come from other parts of the world church?

Can you think of ways in which your church might better reflect their experiences in its prayer and worship?

Perhaps I have gone on quite long enough about the economic and political aspects of the global and local. What about issues close to your own mission as a particular kind of Christian, a professional? I have talked about the social and cultural impact of globalisation on our local communities and the ways in which local struggles against injustice can be waged through global communications and networks. However, as you have repeatedly pointed out, clergy claim to be more than just social workers! Where does religion come into all this?

A universal message

I do not possess your depth of knowledge about the various Christian churches or denominations but, for a start, I believe that they have a universal message to people throughout the world. Missionaries may be criticised for their activities in Africa and elsewhere, but they have operated in the conviction that the Christian message is not just for some local community but for everyone. Consequently, the various denominations have organised themselves on a national and international scale and now they can make use of global communications to take their message anywhere. If Rupert Murdoch can boast that he has the means to beam *Dallas* to Indian villagers through his satellite network, then the Christian churches can propagate a more profound message to the same people. (I may be wrong here but my impression is that so far it has been the more 'conservative' or 'fundamentalist' Protestant groups which have exploited the opportunities of evangelism through radio and television. Perhaps this generalisation could also be applied to the Roman Catholic Church.)

EXERCISE
The World Wide Web is an economical way for churches to communicate their message far and wide. If your local church has set up a website, what message does it communicate?

At whom should church websites be aimed?

Of course mission is no longer understood as just a one-way enterprise, from the First World to the rest. It helps to think of the church in global terms. It is worth remembering, for example, that the majority of Christians in the world are black and poor. Christian churches form a larger group, per capita, in whole areas of Asia and Africa and South America than they do in Europe. This is bound to change our underlying view of the church and its mission.

The issues of power, resistance, standardisation and diversity which I have raised during this letter are integral to the churches' mission. Many of my anthropological colleagues have accused Christian missionaries of promoting alien western values, destroying indigenous ways of life, colluding with colonial and neo-colonial institutions and using schools, hospitals and clerical institutions to buy the faith of people in Third and Fourth World countries. I do not take such a bleak picture of missionary activity, and it is evident that Christian converts have not abandoned many of their traditional customs as repeated missionary blasts in Africa against polygamy, magic and witchcraft affirm.

EXERCISE
📖 **Read Acts 2:5–13.** This forms part of the story of the first Christian Pentecost. It tells the story of how the disciples were able to communicate with a 'global audience'. Luke includes an extensive list of place names in order to underline the fact that individuals from all over the known world are hearing the gospel. In this case the hearers would have been predominantly Jewish, but as the Book of Acts progresses the gospel is proclaimed to the wider Gentile world (see, for example, Acts 10:35). The reader may be intended to pick up echoes of the Tower of Babel story, the first Christian Pentecost in effect reversing the curse of Babel.   ▶▶

Should the story of Pentecost be taken as theological support for globalisation? Why or why not?

What might the theological opportunities of globalisation be?

Christian diversity and contest

However, anthropologists and clergy also know that religion, as officially defined, is not the same as people's everyday belief and practice in whatever part of the world one thinks of. Christian experts like yourself may tell us what to do and believe, and you can use global communications to promote conformity to official teaching. We, on the other hand, can use our own power to resist those teachings and to promote a diversity which is a continual challenge to your authority. Sometimes this struggle may not be obvious, since 'ordinary' Christians may not want to tell you what they really believe and do. Yet anyone who is a sensitive pastor will know the reality of uncertainty and equivocation in people's minds over issues where religious teaching is very clear and unequivocal. I personally believe that it is through these competing processes of standardisation and diversity that change takes place within Christianity.

Anyway this internal struggle can be acted out on a global stage as, indeed, we could observe with the recent contest inside the Church of England concerning the ordination of women as priests. News of this struggle was beamed across the world and we heard about how other Anglican communities or associates had approached this issue. (In some parts of the USA the Episcopal Church had ordained women priests for many years.) We learned about struggles between clergy and congregation within local communities. Even the village where I grew up in Sussex made news because of a fight between the vicar and his congregation over his opposition to the ordination of the parish's female deacon.

Other Christian churches inevitably became involved as public figures such as Conservative MPs left the Church of England for the Roman Catholic Church, for example. Information about the Pope's attitude toward female priests was eagerly sought as the dispute crossed local and national boundaries and became disseminated across the world through the global communications network.

EXERCISE

How might the church in Britain benefit from an awareness of Christian thinking and practice in other parts of the world, such as North America, Asia, Africa and Latin America?

Some Christians criticised the 1998 Lambeth Conference for its relatively conservative stance on issues of human sexuality. Some commentators attributed this conservatism to the influence of Third and Fourth World bishops at the Conference, which itself reflected the numerical ascendancy of Third and Fourth World Anglicanism. How might the Anglican Church, and other denominations, best encourage a diversity of voices to be heard? How might its different constituencies best 'speak the truth in love' (Ephesians 4:15) to each other?

The capacity of globalisation to allow a diversity of voices to compete is becomingly increasingly apparent and raises important challenges for contemporary Christian thinking and practice. In the past theology and theological education have usually reflected a European or North American bias. They have traditionally dealt with the issues that arise in European and North American contexts and considered the way that Europeans and North Americans deal with them. Increasingly this provincialism has been challenged by writers from Asia, Africa and Latin America. Women and minorities in Europe and North America have also drawn attention to the value assumptions that invariably underlie these traditional approaches.

As Christians develop an increasingly global perspective they cannot avoid an awareness of other religious faiths. Post-war immigration patterns have meant that sizeable communities of other religious faiths are now well established in Britain. The awareness of the voices of other religious faiths is therefore an important aspect of globalisation and Christians cannot avoid the theological and practical challenges that it brings.

Not surprisingly, the processes I have described, as internal struggles are acted out on a global stage, do not apply solely to Christians. Events happening among Bradford's Pakistani Muslims over *The Satanic Verses* by Salman Rushdie (1988) were connected through media reports with riots and protests in Bombay, Karachi and Teheran. The death of Sikh 'extremists' at Amritsar's Golden Temple in the Indian state of Punjab have repercussions for struggles among Sikhs living in Southall, Chicago and Vancouver.

What I find most interesting about these events is the way in which religious affiliation is defined through political struggle. People are not being judged by others or, perhaps, themselves, in terms of their religious observance; rather they are being labelled according to their (frequently unwitting) involvement in political conflicts at local or more global levels. For example, Protestants or Catholics in Belfast have been murdered not principally because they attend chapel or mass but because they live in a certain locality, went to a particular school and have a particular name. They may be an agnostic or atheist in terms of belief but that will not determine whether they live or die.

So we are in an age where the politics of identity shapes the way people understand religious affiliation. Globalisation enables this politics to flourish across the world and it presents a challenge, I would suggest, to the way church leaders like yourself understand the world of Christian mission. Does the message of universal love require us to challenge fundamentalist identities which encourage the persecution of others, whether these 'others' belong to other Christian denominations or to non-Christian faiths? What do we do about murderous attacks on Christians by people described as 'Hindu fundamentalists' in India or 'Muslim fundamentalists' in Pakistan?

In the global village, people are increasingly aware of alternatives. They know that their particular values, beliefs and moral principles are not necessarily shared by others on this planet, or even within their own society. People recognise that their ideas of the good life, their ideas of what is right, and even their ideas of God, have been strongly shaped by the society in which they have been raised. It is apparent that their ideas and value commitments are, to a large extent, man-made and not God-given. Globalisation has made available a cornucopia of choices, undreamt of by previous generations.

People react to this vast array of choice in different ways. On the one hand, some people may seek to reinforce their particular identity, as they vigorously define themselves over against the alternatives and assert their distinctiveness. Religious fundamentalists, for instance, identify themselves as sole possessors of truth and deny that truth can be found elsewhere. On the other hand, people may become bewildered and find it difficult to cope with so much choice. Globalisation relativises people's values and beliefs and introduces a note of doubt: 'Have

I made the right choice?' ... 'Is there a right choice?' ... 'Might I believe something different if I lived somewhere different?' ... 'Might I believe something different tomorrow?' Globalisation also tends to relativise the great religious traditions, including Christianity. Religious education in British schools, operating along multi-cultural lines, arguably encourages children to treat Christianity as just one faith amongst many. It may also have helped to encourage a 'pick and mix' approach within contemporary spirituality whereby, for instance, an individual may simultaneously draw on medieval mysticism, Celtic spirituality, Feng Shui, yoga and indigenous North American spirituality.

But it is always dangerous to generalise about globalisation. Although Christianity may find itself marginalised by globalisation, there are also tendencies within globalisation that might propel Christianity back to centre stage. Globalisation may have de-secularising implications for religion. Living in the global village, we have begun to think in international and global terms. In the past, people tended to think more narrowly, in terms of national needs and objectives. Ever since people saw the first images of planet earth taken from outer space they have been painfully aware of the fragility of our globe and the fact that we sink or swim together. Environmental disasters, such as the nuclear accident at Chernobyl or the BSE crisis, cannot be contained within the borders of a nation-state and may pose a threat to the whole human race. We increasingly tend to have a sense of commonality at the global level. We think in terms of humanity and of human, rather than merely national, issues. Our quest is no longer just to discover what binds society together; we are also interested in what might bind our globe together.

This begins to counterbalance the tendency of globalisation to relativise. If the world is to survive, individuals cannot simply be free to assert their right to believe and act however they wish. They need to take into account universal norms of what it means to be humane. Here religion has a chance to come into its own, as a unique cultural resource dealing with the human being per se. Advances in medical science mean that nation-states are increasingly having to legislate about profound life and death issues. Faced with moral dilemmas surrounding such practices as euthanasia, abortion and human genetic modification, it is significant that nation-states increasingly turn to philosophers and theologians for advice. Such issues are not simply to be settled on political and pragmatic grounds; they raise deep questions about the nature and purpose of human life.

If religion is to have an impact on global issues, and not merely to be pushed to the margins, it may need to speak with a more unified voice. The 1993 'Declaration Toward a Global Ethic' by the Parliament of the World's Religions was one attempt to do this (Küng and Kuschel, 1993). Meeting in Chicago, representatives of the world's religions signed a statement of what they 'already have in common now in the ethical sphere' (p. 8). The Declaration has not been without its critics. Some have argued that it is too 'western'. Others have criticised the Parliament for including neo-pagans. But, whatever the limitations, it is surely an important spur towards developing a common ethic for humankind.

Let me end on a more upbeat note by quoting you the conclusion of an article in *Christian Century* by Barnes (1991).

> Globalization involves the possibility of a gracious recovery and recasting of the catholicity of the faith. The very term suggests that the church, amid a diverse and pluralistic yet singular and increasingly unified world, can move beyond the fissiparous tendencies of sectarianism and dogmatism and beyond the mere pragmatism of adjusting to the demands of the moment. It thus requires a new quest for excellence: a renewed dedication to mission, ecumenicity, dialogue and justice; and fresh approaches to learning and teaching. Above all, it calls for courage and wisdom to speak of God in ways that signal the divine universality, reform the church, and guide the reconstruction of civilization.

Powerful stuff, don't you think? I am not sure that globalisation can be given such high-faluting credentials. However, let's discuss these claims in the light of my sociological preoccupations when we meet.

Best wishes,

John

EXERCISE

Is it right to be this optimistic about globalisation? Note the arguments for and against such optimism.

Postscript

EXERCISE
  📖 **Read Matthew 28:18–20.**

What does the passage say about globalisation?

📖 **Read Acts 17:26.**

What does this passage say about globalisation?

How new an idea is globalisation?

Perhaps global thinking is not an entirely new phenomenon after all. Already, in the ancient world, Greek philosophy operated within global parameters and sought to include all human beings within its frame of reference. Christianity understood itself as a religion for every human being. It recognised that there was only one human race (Acts 17:26), that the gospel was for all the peoples of the world (Matthew 28:18–20), and that potentially anyone might put their faith in Jesus Christ. During the last two millennia the practice of pilgrimage has helped to keep alive people's sense of belonging to a world church with global aspirations. Both for those who travelled to holy sites as pilgrims, and for those who heard their stories when they returned, the pilgrimage was an important means of raising people's awareness of the wider human community. Pilgrims often travelled overseas as well as in their own lands. This has included pilgrimages to the Holy Land since the early days of the Christian calendar.

Further reading

Albrow M and King E (1990), *Globalization, Knowledge and Society*, London, Sage.

Eade, J (1997), *Living in a Global City*, London, Routledge.

Featherstone, M (ed.), (1990), *Global Culture: nationalism, globalization and modernity*, London, Sage.

Giddens, A (1999), *Globalization: Reith Lectures 1999* (forthcoming).

Robertson, R (1992), *Globalization*, London, Sage.

3. THE TIES THAT BIND

Introduction

In this chapter we shall:
- explore geographic and economic communities;
- analyse some of the differences between modern and traditional social forms;
- discuss some of the different values associated with community.

Reflecting on experience
Make a note whenever you hear someone refer to 'the community' and record what they mean by it. Make a glossary of these meanings at the end of a week.

Note how politicians use the term.

Ideas and visions of community

Any consideration of *community* must begin by asking whether community is something in the head or whether there are real social formations that we can identify as communities. The *idea* of a community is powerful, as evidenced by the wide range of circumstances in which it is deployed. Such potent ideas can have powerful social consequences. But this very potency is aided by the flexibility with which the term may be used. Borland, Fevre and Denny (1992) in their study of nationalism and community in North West Wales have shown how four different concepts of community may be applied to the same geographical area, each embodying different variants of Welsh nationalism. These concepts range from the idea of 'the open community', according to which anyone who lives and works in Wales can be a member of the Welsh community, to the idea of 'the racially closed community', according to which only those who possess the Welsh 'spirit' can belong to the community. In this case different ideas of community are likely to indicate quite different political programmes. Ideas of community do not necessarily remain in the mind; they can have concrete effects. The concept of 'the racially closed community', for instance, has been linked to fire bombings of English settlers. 'Community' is therefore a highly contested term and, in the same context, may be imagined in different ways. It is not a given.

Important sociological debates surround the term 'community'. A contrast between community (*Gemeinschaft*) and society or association (*Gesellschaft*) was developed in the late nineteenth century by Ferdinand Tönnies in summarising the differences between the typical social relations of pre-industrial society and modern industrial societies (see Tönnies, 1957). In his community/society dichotomy Tönnies attempted to capture certain essential differences between industrial society and what had gone before. As societies had modernised, human relationships had become less emotionally cohesive, more superficial, less enduring and less fulfilling. Local loyalties had given way to the impersonal contracts of large-scale industrial society.

Communities have been characterised as small-scale and homogenous, with relationships based upon face-to-face contact. You could know everyone in the community. This knowing extended across generations: my father knew your father and your grandfather knew mine. People therefore were judged by others on the basis of who they were and who their antecedents were rather than what they were. Whatever they may have achieved they remained trapped in an ascribed status, as their mother's daughter or their father's son. Behaviour was judged by traditional values; you were measured against the standards of your forebears.

By contrast the modern city is characterised by the mass, the crowd and by anonymity. I only meet you once as a bus driver or a magistrate. I know nothing else about you as a person, only the role in which I meet you. We never meet again. People may join trades unions or the Rotarians if they meet the criteria for membership. Membership is sustained by paying dues and obeying the rules of the organisation. Members may leave if they wish. Mobilisation is around interests not kinship, and the political party is the typical association of the modern world. Your social status is defined by such memberships, by your qualifications and achievements. Nobody knows or cares where you came from or who your mother and grandmother were. Behaviour is judged according to rules and ultimately by law, both of which may be changed by recognised formal processes.

EXERCISE

📖 **Read Galatians 3:26–28.** Paul offers a vision of Christian community in which *achieved*, rather than *ascribed*, status is all important. Membership of the community comes through baptism and through the response of faith in Christ. Ascribed social status, by virtue of being Jew or Gentile, slave or free person, man or woman, is no longer important.

To what extent is Paul's radically egalitarian notion of Christian community evident in churches you have known?

The modern city is where people can get on. You make your own fortune, define who you are and rise and fall according to ability, luck and the power of others to facilitate or hinder your progress. It is the air of the city that sets men and women free from the restrictions and limitations of life in the village. The price to be paid is the alienation and despair that can arise from being alone and without friends.

In the community you can never rise above your ascribed status, never be anything other than others say you are. In the city you can do what you like with whomever you like and strive to become whatever you wish. The community then is narrow and restrictive as well as potentially supportive; the city is liberating and alienating. Of course, both these accounts are caricatures and incorporate moral judgements.

Ambivalence towards the merits of the small community and the big city is seen throughout the history of Europe. We see it today in students and colleagues who enjoy the support of parents and take pleasure in going back to their home town to meet old friends. But they would never dream of going back to work in the place from which they came. The major cities are powerful attractions.

There is often a large degree of nostalgia attached to concepts of community. A romantic myth comes into play of a close-knit community in which everyone knew each other, where everyone was ready to help each other, and where modern problems of delinquency and vandalism just did not exist. The idealised community is perhaps the medieval village, where people might spend virtually their whole lives. Here they worked, ate, slept, loved, prayed and played together.

In a society of high geographical mobility and rapid change, the church can be a much-needed source of close friendships and supportive networks. In their recent study of church leaving and returning, *Gone but not Forgotten*, Philip Richter and Leslie J Francis (1998) conclude that some church leaving results from disappointment at the failure of the church to provide, at least in the leaver's estimation, a proper sense of belonging. They highlight four areas of perceived imbalance within churches that can motivate someone to leave: imbalances between involvement and passivity, intimacy and anonymity, plant and congregation size, and inclusiveness and exclusiveness. Individuals are prone to leave if they perceive the church to be tipping the balance too far in what they regard as the wrong direction (chapter 10).

EXERCISE

When some people speak of the church as a 'community' they seem to be envisaging a return to a golden age when people's leisure hours revolved around the church and when people could speak of themselves as almost 'living there'. Would you welcome a return to such patterns of church involvement? Would it fit into your understanding of the church as a community?

Nostalgia, however, often entails putting on rose-coloured spectacles. Village life was by no means always utopian. It could be a rustic prison for its inhabitants. Life could be stifling and stunting. There was often little tolerance for outsiders or for those who refused to conform. Individuals were born into their station in life and there they were expected to remain. As a verse of the hymn 'All things bright and beautiful' put it: 'The rich man in his castle, the poor man at his gate; God made them high and lowly, and ordered their estate.'

Concepts of community are often associated with implicit value judgements about what is the good life. Nostalgia for rural utopia is commonly expressed by those who value stability, order and tradition. Others, however, would reject the medieval village as rural dystopia. It is true that everyone may have known everyone else in the medieval village, but that meant that nobody could escape the community's all-seeing eye. Conformity, rather than individual autonomy, was valued. Such a community could be a claustrophobic and oppressive place to be.

Harvey Cox, the Christian theologian, has been a radical critic of the conservative concept of community. He actively favoured the 'secular city' for the freedom, independence and autonomy it offered, by virtue of the more anonymous nature of secular urban life. In the 1960s Cox made the controversial claim that the exercise of Christian freedom required the degree of freedom of choice offered by life in the secular city. The very anonymity of the city provided an environment in which Christian freedom was most possible. In his book *The Secular City*, Cox (1965) actively welcomed the loss of a sense of traditional community in the context of modern city life. Here he described how shocked some clergy were when they realised that many newly arrived apartment residents had no interest in making contact with their new neighbours or in participating in church or community groups. He commented: 'The ministers had wanted to develop a kind of village togetherness among people, one of whose main reasons for moving to high-rise apartments is to escape the relationships enforced on them by the lack of anonymity of the village ... the ministers had made the mistake of confusing a pre-urban ethos with the Christian concept of *koinonia*' – the New Testament term for togetherness or fellowship (Cox, 1965, p. 44).

We romanticise the past. Life in the small community is associated with rural life in a bygone age. But it was life in the countryside that was described as 'nasty, brutish and short'. Anyone with illusions about the history of the English countryside should read *The Labourer* by John and Barbara Hammond (1995).

EXERCISE
What are some of the values you would want to encourage in your church and other communities?

Christians, like other people, generally make certain underlying value judgements when they use the term 'community'. This is natural and unproblematic, provided that these value assumptions have been subjected to the scrutiny of the Christian gospel. As David Clark (1973, p. 193) has suggested: 'The Christian gospel is very much about (people's) quest, alongside (those) of religious belief or none, for solidarity and significance, and the Christian is called to take these basic essentials of community more, not less, seriously than others.'

What kind of values might Christians want to encourage in their church and other communities? They might look for a community that is, on the one hand, warm and close-knit, and yet is, on the other hand, neither narrow nor exclusive. They might look for community that offers individuals a sense of personal significance and self-worth, combined with growth in autonomy. 'Community at its richest is found in those social groupings where (the individual) experiences the most intensive and comprehensive degree of solidarity consistent with the realisation of the autonomy of each' (Clark, 1973, p. 193). This will entail avoiding certain sub-Christian forms of community, such as the community for the exclusive few, the community that derives its vitality from hatred of a common enemy, the suffocating, stifling community that demands dull conformity, or the community that expects uncritical obedience to its leadership. The church is called to embody and nurture a radically different vision of human togetherness, as a distinctive 'moral community' (Gill, 1992).

Geographic and economic community studies

We need very clear definitions. The 'true' community is often identified with the rural but as we will see communities are not necessarily rural. They may be urban also. 'Community' has been discovered in the modern world, both inside large cities and in rural settlements. It belongs to the literature of both industrialisation and development.

Oscar Lewis wrote a series of studies about the life of peasants who moved to Mexico City and further afield to the USA. The best known of these are *The Children of Sanchez* (1961), *Pedro Martinez* (1964) and *La Vida* (1965); these studies build on important earlier work, which includes *Five Families* (1959). Lewis showed how the culture of the Mexican peasant could be adapted to the city to ensure the survival of the migrant, albeit on the margins of the economy and society of the big city. Similar ideas were developed in the study of African migrant workers, a notable work in this vein being Philip Mayer's *Townsmen or Tribesmen* (1961).

It was from Lewis's work that the idea of a 'culture of poverty' was derived. In *A Study of Slum Culture*, Lewis (1968, pp. 5–6) wrote:

The culture of poverty is both an adaptation and a reaction of the

poor to their marginal position in a class-stratified, highly individu-
ated, capitalist society. ... Once it comes into existence, it tends to
perpetuate itself from generation to generation because of its effect on
the children.

This idea was to be interpreted and modified into an argument about
the way in which poor people developed strategies for survival which
they then transmitted to their children. Such ideas were later adapted to
suit the agenda of the New Right in finding ways to break the cycle of
transmitted deprivation or the culture of dependency. It enabled them
to locate the blame for poverty in the family. As an intellectual exercise
it came to nothing but remains a powerful political theme. Serious
scholars are nonetheless coming to appreciate the importance of 'the
strength of weak ties and the weakness of strong ties', especially in the
contexts of European and transnational migrations, where those who
are less deeply embedded in kin and culture are more able to move,
innovate and adapt.

In the UK there were a series of post-war community studies, of
which the best known are those of the Institute of Community Studies,
although similar work was being undertaken in the University of Liverpool. One of the most famous, *Family and Kinship in East London* by
Young and Willmott (1957), was followed by studies of the East-enders
in the London periphery. Even as Young and Willmott wrote, the localities they were describing were being transformed. New forms of community and new means of mobilising kinship had to be created in new
circumstances.

EXERCISE
Think back five years. What was different then about the locality in
which you live? How have these changes affected you personally?

What did they discover in Bethnal Green? They found, in contrast to
press accounts (later attributed to sociologists) of the decline of the
family, that family and kinship flourished. The network of kinship
spread out to link families across the geographical area of Bethnal Green
and immediately beyond.

The density of the social networks was such that Young and Willmott
found that in a street of 59 households, 38 had relatives in other

households in the street. They found 45 couples with 1,691 relatives of whom over one half lived in Bethnal Green or adjacent boroughs. Couples had an average of thirteen relatives within the borough.

Kinship worked. 'Mum' was a key figure in finding homes for married daughters. Mothers and aunts provided child care and care in sickness. They were themselves cared for in old age by the younger generation of women. Sons followed fathers into work and the council reserved certain jobs for the widows of council employees.

During the same period in British sociology a series of studies was being conducted by Littlejohn, Frankenberg, Williams and others in the countryside. All described localities with long-established families, rich associational lives, mutual aid and a sense of 'belonging'. But these small societies were also stratified and the pattern of cross-cutting loyalties made conflict and change difficult to handle. All the communities were experiencing changes derived from external influences beyond their control.

EXERCISE

📖 **Read 1 Corinthians 1:10–12 and then 1:4–9.** Paul is writing to a Christian community torn apart by internal conflict but, significantly, he does not treat his opponents as if they are outside the community. He gives thanks to God for them (v. 4).

Is conflict a normal and healthy part of Christian community?

The stability and longevity of communities is very problematic. Part of the myth of community seems to be a belief in a golden age in the none too distant past. But although a village may have been mentioned in the Domesday book it is unlikely that it has been a single community in every subsequent year. Frankenberg's Glynceiroig was suffering from the closure of quarries, Williams' Gosforth was about to experience an influx of people connected with the nuclear power industry. Bethnal Green was the object of slum-clearance policies and the docks and associated economic activities were in rapid decline.

All of these earlier studies have been summarised in Frankenberg's (1969) *Communities in Britain*. A critique of British community studies, *Community Life* by Crow and Allan (1994), reviews a much larger number of community studies including those written after Frankenberg's volume was published.

When researching for his book *Pitmen, Preachers and Politics* (1974) in Durham in the mid-1960s, Moore often sat talking with elderly men and women. Occasionally he would be joined by another elderly person visiting the friend. Men and women, 80 years old or more, had been at school together in the village, knew one anothers' parents and grand-parents, married one anothers' sisters and friends and had mutual friends who died in the Great War. They exchanged reminiscences of people who had been born in the first half of the nineteenth century but were known to them as children. They had probably seen one another almost every day, or at least once a week, for seventy years or more in the same locality. They closed their friendships at one anothers' funerals. Such encounters were deeply moving for the (then) young sociologist, but will future sociologists encounter relations of such long continuity?

Whether communities are real or not the 'village in the mind' is important in understanding change in rural areas. Ray Pahl in the 1960s studied commuter villages in the outer London fringe. Here he found people who were pursuing a rural idyll, a desire to establish 'roots' for their children in a healthy environment. They were highly committed to a vision of rurality and community, which seldom extended to sending their children to the local school. They were opposed to council house building and indifferent to the provision of bus services, both vital to truly local people. Pahl shows that the middle-class incomers were seeking a particular kind of society characterised by idealised social relationships in which everyone knew their place and, especially, honoured the incomers' high status. The villages were already differen-tiated and stratified; the incomers provoked further divisions. What the incomers were looking for, they effectively destroyed by their presence.

Nearly all the studies mentioned so far have been of communities that were in some sense economic communities. People were there because they had work. Lack of work leads to population decline, the most able leave, the remainder become residualised and marginalised. Perhaps those most closely integrated into the community are most at risk of being unable to move. A corollary to this is that people with the strongest community ties in a declining area may be tied to increasing poverty. The community may still be a trap and strong ties may weaken individual social actors.

One of the most interesting features of Bethnal Green was that kinship *functioned*, it was a little welfare state supporting people in adversity. Jobs and housing were both scarce resources; kinship was important in acquiring them and later in restricting newcomers' access to them. Kinship provided mutual support for illness, childbirth and childcare in a system that pre-dated the postwar welfare state. In the countryside mutual aid was important in fulfilling the cycle of agricultural tasks. Conflict was also important in the communities studied and kinship did not always provide the basis for resolving conflict, indeed, it could amplify conflict.

An example of such conflict was provided by a deeply divided small Scottish fishing port. The fisherfolk were held in the lowest esteem, and 'respectable' members of the community seldom met fishermen and they looked down on them. The church of the town's élite was once the venue for televised hymn-singing on Sunday evening. The church was decorated with floats and nets for the occasion and presented as the church of 'a fishing community'.

EXERCISE
Imagine *Songs of Praise* coming to the highest status church in your town. How might the congregation appropriate the culture and values of the most deprived section of the population for the occasion?

Communities do not happen, they are not given, they are made. It was coping with poverty and uncertain employment in Bethnal Green (and Mexico City) that made communities. The female networks were especially important, not because women are necessarily more sociable, but because the women of Bethnal Green belonged to a generation which lacked even the health insurance that husbands may have had if the husbands were fortunate enough to be skilled workers. The women bore a domestic burden, perhaps in addition to paid employment, and only had other women to turn to for support. In the immediate post-Beveridge debates about the welfare state the conflicts of interests between men and women were very clear. Men wanted a 'family wage' and saw Family Allowances as a means of suppressing their wages. Eleanor Rathbone and others argued that paying men a 'family wage' was no guarantee that wives and children would not fall into need.

Organised labour wanted a welfare state that incorporated women's dependence upon men, and to a large extent that is what they got.

Communitarianism

Recent present-day attempts to reformulate the notion of the welfare state have tended to use the language of 'community', albeit sometimes pragmatically in order to justify reductions in government spending. The views of communitarian sociologist Amitai Etzioni are known to have influenced President Clinton and Prime Minister Tony Blair. In his book *The Spirit of Community*, Etzioni (1995) argued that a balance is needed between individual and collective rights. Society depends on its members' acceptance of mutual obligations and of a core of common ethical values, such as 'no one in our community should be left to starve'. Such values help to cement society together. Communities, as well as individuals, have responsibilities and rights. Communities have the right, for instance, to make divorce more difficult if, as a result, children will be raised as more balanced and responsible members of society. Society has the right to insist that those in receipt of welfare payments should be willing to work, to be retrained, or to undertake community service. Etzioni has criticised both the permissive individualism of the 1960s and the greedy acquisitiveness of the Thatcherite 1980s. His communitarian vision entails retreat from over-dependence on the state and revival of the institutions that lie between the state and the individual, such as family, neighbourhood, school and church, in order that talk of individual rights and freedoms may be balanced by talk of community rights and mutual obligation.

Etzioni recognised the importance of those institutions that stand between the individual and the state: the effects of the failure to create such institutions is painfully clear in Eastern Europe. In the UK also we can see the effects of the decline of employment and the consequent collapse of working-class communities. We see that the destruction of trades unions and the stresses upon families that have been impoverished both destroy social solidarity and undermine social stability. The loss of solidarity may be important in making us all vulnerable to problems which find a range of expressions, from despair and delinquency to addiction and suicide. A radical rebuilding of social solidarity may be called for. If this is communitarianism then who can be against it? But, given its attractiveness to Clinton and Blair, communitarianism plainly has a very conservative aspect.

In a world where the most influential forces acting upon us are global, corporate and international, communitarianism invites us to think and act locally. This will encourage ascriptive rather than needs-based responses to problems and is likely to promote social closure and exclusion. This will create gaps in provision which either *cannot* be met locally, because of insufficient resources, or *will not* be met, because they are the needs of less popular groups. Wider debates about the rational and orderly allocation of national resources become local disputes over limited resources. Furthermore, the adoption of a communitarian stance enables the state and the corporate sector to disengage, while at the same time both obscuring their responsibilities for the problems that people face and reducing people's capacities to deal with the problems. Communitarianism may, therefore, come to represent an abrogation of the collective responsibilities and obligations of members of the wider society to one another.

Further reading

Most of the early post-war community studies are summarised (very briefly) in Frankenberg's book, and these and more recent studies in Crow and Allan. You should use these two volumes to lead you into particular studies that you wish to follow up. You will be tapping into an especially rich vein of British sociology.

Crow, G and Allan, G (1994), *Community Life: an introduction to local social relations*, London, Harvester Wheatsheaf.

Frankenberg, R (1969), *Communities in Britain: social life in town and country*, Harmondsworth, Penguin.

4. DIVIDED WE STAND?

Introduction

In this chapter we shall:
- explore communities of interest;
- analyse community cleavage;
- discuss the view that communities are made, not given.

Reflecting on experience
What networks do you belong to? What networks do other church members belong to?

Do you belong to non-church networks? Do other church members belong to non-church networks?

How far, if at all, do these overlap and intersect with church networks?

Communities of interest

So far we have discussed communities largely defined in terms of their geographical location. This definition is sensible because people may live their lives among a relatively geographically limited population. Interaction with people who are 'somewhere else' is difficult, but by no means impossible.

But people do not automatically form a community simply because they happen to live in close proximity to each other. This is a common myth that has inspired many town planners. Town planners have tended to subdivide new towns and large housing estates into local neighbourhoods in the belief that these would form meaningful social units. One critic has spoken of 'that flavour of ideological beatification' attaching to belief in the locality community (Dennis, 1968, p. 86). It is not only town planners who have assumed that groups of people or houses automatically form a community. Churches, too, often mistake locality for community. Churches often make quite ambiguous statements about community. They often speak of 'serving the local community' but in the same breath lament the decline of a sense of community. Churches seldom ask themselves whether there really is a local community and whether experience of community may have taken new forms in contemporary society. Unless such questions are addressed, then 'community' is a redundant word. It could equally well be replaced by 'society' or 'public'.

In today's society community is often better expressed in terms of 'network' rather than 'territory'. Individuals belong to sets of networks. People may derive a sense of community from more than one network. An individual might, for instance, belong to a family, a company, a pub, a choir, a leisure centre, a parents' association, and a church. Some of these networks may overlap with each other. Members of the choir might play squash together at the leisure centre. Other networks may be totally distinct. Individuals may commute some distance to their workplace and never meet any of their colleagues in the other networks to which they belong. In a society characterised by a good deal of career-led geographic mobility people do not always have the time or inclination to put down local roots.

Some networks may never involve face-to-face contact. The Internet has made it possible to belong to virtual cyber communities and to communicate with groups of people from many different parts of the globe without ever meeting them in person. Viewers of religious television programmes, such as *Songs of Praise*, may have a sense of belonging to a virtual worshipping community, whilst never meeting their co-worshippers. They may even prefer this to church attendance.

These new forms of community raise fresh issues for churches. If people are today less used to living in close-knit, face-to-face communities, some people may be alienated by churches that expect displays of emotional intensity. They may prefer to attend more formal and less participatory worship, such as early morning eucharist according to *The Book of Common Prayer* or Evensong. The practice of milling about and affectionately greeting fellow worshippers during the sharing of the Peace may, for instance, be uncomfortable for some. On the other hand, others may be attracted to churches of this type precisely because they are searching for a surrogate close-knit, face-to-face community, which is not offered by any of the other networks to which they belong.

Individual churches may be able to offer both kinds of community, perhaps by having a series of different types of worship each Sunday. Some churches are, however, 'gathered' churches, simply drawing together those of similar persuasion. Although Anglican churches have traditionally operated as inclusive communities, open to any resident of the parish, there has lately been a growing tendency for some parish churches to become gathered churches, attracting merely evangelicals or charismatics or Anglo-Catholics, for instance. Those who do not fit the given category and the more nominal churchgoers of the parish can feel excluded from such gathered churches.

If networks have today become more important than locality-based communities in many people's lives, the Church of England's focus on the parish may need to be re-examined. Church planting may need to be seen not simply in terms of taking the church's mission to newly developed housing areas, but also in terms of engaging with specific networks.

We also speak of 'communities of interest'. We find networks of mutual support in non-geographical contexts in organisations like Alcoholics Anonymous, in women's refuges and in trades unions. These are formal organisations with defined objectives but they are all marked by camaraderie rooted in shared experiences. The affection of the kinship network is found in an association where there are no ties of blood or marriage. Elements of such mutuality may even be found in 'the heroin community'.

EXERCISE

📖 **Read James 2:15.** Kinship language is used here to describe members of the Christian community.

Do you ever think of your fellow churchgoers in these terms? What difference, if any, would such language make? Do you ever think of Christians beyond your local church in these terms?

There are few sociological accounts of life in women's refuges but the available studies suggest that most were established consciously as 'alternative' institutions in which women could be free both from male dominance and violence and from the formal constraints of professional case-work. The refuges were not free of internal conflict but they were marked by a strong sense of shared female experience and woman-to-woman solidarity. Thus Dale and Foster (1986, pp. 167–168) wrote as follows:

> After two or three days when you've been there and you see another woman come in you try to help her, like you've been helped. You can fit in and discuss things and you know that you're not the only person in the world that's been battered, or even gone through a bad time and it sort of helps you in that way.

Here the community may be located in one small building, and it is bound together by shared experiences, the need for privacy and defence. The community creates its locality. The one-house community may not be economically self-supporting (any more than most of the traditional localities studied) but there may be virtual self-sufficiency at the level of values and emotions.

We also speak, more loosely, of the 'lesbian and gay community', suggesting that sexual identities are created and sustained in social contexts and implying that persons sharing similar identities recognise one another and are likely to provide support and sympathy for one another. But we are beginning to move away from the idea of community with which we began in the previous chapter. We will consider the implications of this below.

We also recognise ethnic communities: twelve million migrants from outside Europe have been located in the European Union. Until recently it was the European *Community*, a term that provokes a series of debates that we may ignore for our present purposes. For many the bonds of kin and village were the basis on which they found housing, jobs and emotional support in an alien land. Families were reunited much later, often in the face of considerable local hostility expressed through immigration laws intended to reduce the chances of family reunion. Religion also functioned to hold the wider group together. When I was sitting in a service at a Sikh Gurdwara with a Punjabi friend in the mid 1960s he leant across to me and said, 'Here I can almost feel that I am at home again.' At that time, for him, home was not where he lived and if he identified himself with a territory it was not territory in the UK.

Within the ethnic minority population we see the forging of new identities and new communities, notably 'the black community'. In this case it is very obvious that identities are contingent and that communities are 'made, not given'. At home I'm a Bengali or a Kittician or even British or Scouser. If I am Afro-Caribbean I may have aspired to be wholly British in my identity. If I am Indian or Bengali I may have seen myself as Hindu or Muslim, but never 'black'. But the hostility and violence of the white population, political stigmatisation and police harassment may make me black.

EXERCISE

The 1991 census asked people to tick one of the following categories: white/ black-Caribbean/ black-African/ black-other/ Indian/ Pakistani/ Bangladeshi/ Chinese/ other ethnic group.

Karim was born in Tanzania (East Africa), as were his parents and grandparents, but he is of Asian descent and a British national. How should Karim fill in the census form? Do any of these categories fit him? What might this tell us about Karim's sense of communal belonging?

An influential study has demonstrated this process of 'making' a community. The title *Newham: the forging of a black community* makes it clear that a community is hammered into its particular form. The authors show how in the early days of settlement in Newham black and Asian people were radicalised by the experience of discrimination in work and housing. The collapse of unionised work (in an area not far from Bethnal Green) left the area without trades unions and with little base for working-class organisation. This left an opening for the National Front and the British National Party.

Local people became the victims of racial attacks but when they defended themselves they were arrested and prosecuted whilst their attackers went free. The Newham Monitoring Project (1991, pp. 36–37) made the following point:

> The very intensity of the racism at all levels – in the police force, in the judiciary and in the growth of the far Right – was pulling the communities together, binding them, out of sheer necessity, to fight a common racism and throwing up a leadership that was constantly on

the move, from defence campaign to defence campaign, making contacts and setting up organisations.

The mobilisation united people across age and gender divisions (Newham Monitoring Project, 1991, pp. 41 and 53). There were therefore divisions to be overcome, older people tended to be more concerned with 'proper channels' whilst younger people (bearing the brunt of attacks) wanted immediate action. When mobilisation brought success in the form of grants there was every potential for interests to be set against one another and for 'ethnic' groups to be in competition for resources. But what was 'forged' in response to shared adversity was a 'black community' and plainly it needed to be worked upon to be sustained as a single community.

Community divisions

Community is contingent and subject to stresses and strains from external and internal sources that could divide as well as unite. Outside agencies in the form of central and local government and the voluntary sector may, in bringing resources to a local population, change the community structure by providing the means by which networks of patron-client relations may be established and internal differences of interest amplified. The problems of sustaining a black community highlight the problems of sustaining any community. It also highlights the folly of using the term 'community' uncritically.

My experience with clergy and lay training is that the latter often need the idea of community in order to homogenise populations characterised by marked differences of interest or life chances. Lay people are much more reluctant to take sides and when asked, for example, 'Are you for the rich or for the poor?' will either deny the fact of poverty or blame the poor for it. I found it unhelpful then to make the obvious point that they were for the rich and against the poor!

But for most church people it is much easier to refer to your 'community' and avoid facing the deep divisions within your local population. Perhaps the presence of ethnic minority populations has had the additional benefit of making this evasion more difficult.

It is important to be aware of underlying definitions of community with which Christians may be working. Some, for instance, might define community as a group of people, in a given location, with a common set of shared beliefs and values. In that definition there would not seem to be much room for legitimate disagreement, dissent or division concerning the values of the community. Such a concept of community might not allow for a truly multi-cultural and multi-racial society. It might only allow for integration of ethnic minorities into the values of the majority. In that case a different definition of community might need to be developed, recognising that dissent and division may, if handled constructively, be signs of health within a community.

'The community' is a contested idea and often a community, whether it be in Peterhead or Newham, is at its most coherent *against* others. Older Britons sometimes look back with nostalgia to the community spirit engendered by the Second World War and the camaraderie of army life or life in the air-raid shelter during the Blitz. To turn Karl Marx on his head: we may find communities to be things for themselves but not in themselves.

EXERCISE

Is it true that communities become most united against a common enemy?

Should churches ever be united against common enemies?

Outside forces may, however, conspire to prevent communities becoming mobilised around issues of common interest. Those who govern society have often been keen to promote communities based on locality, as part of a 'divide and rule' policy. Such communities are less likely to de-stabilise social order and tend to be less threatening to those with a vested interest in the status quo. The separate development policy in South Africa, involving the creation of separate homelands for different racial groups, was evidently an attempt to shore up South Africa's apartheid system. Similarly, the building in this country of municipal estates for large numbers of the working class has been seen as a tool for controlling this potentially troublesome segment of the population. One nineteenth-century social theorist, T Chalmers, advocated the principle of 'locality', as he termed it, as a useful instrument of civic and religious administration in towns: through the general application of the local system, he claimed, the unmanageable mass which would otherwise form into one impetuous and overwhelming surge against the reigning authority could be split up into fragments (see

Gladstone, 1995). In line with this perspective, one reason why community associations are encouraged on new estates might be because their latent function is to contribute to the stability of society by occupying the time and energy of potential social critics and activists. The practice of dispersing people into separated communities can, therefore, be interpreted as a fundamentally conservative and stabilising factor in society. This is not to accuse the dominant classes of a mass conspiracy, or even to assume a consciously worked-out plan, but it does help to explain why the neighbourhood community idea has a high survival value.

Churches may unwittingly collude with this 'divide and rule' tendency. A church may see its role in terms of lubricating the local community and stimulating a sense of local community spirit. But it may, in the process, fail to identify wider communities of interest with which the local community might need to find common cause. It is important that a community should have sufficient resources and clout for outside authorities to take them seriously. This will sometimes entail forming coalitions with people in other localities with similar problems and interests. A working-class community facing the closure of its principal industry might, for instance, need to form alliances with people in other locations facing similar difficulties, in order to mount an effective response. Sometimes lobbying in places far away from the locality will be necessary in order to influence decisions that will have important repercussions for the local community. Of course in theory, if not always in practice, because the church is not just a local organisation it is wellplaced to empower people and to help them to develop wider networks of common interest.

EXERCISE
📖 **Read Genesis 49:1–28** – Jacob's final blessing for his twelve
    sons, the twelve tribes of Israel. In the Old Testament the
    people of Israel are represented as twelve tribes sharing a com-
    mon genealogical heritage in the patriarchs Abraham, Isaac
    and Jacob.

What do you understand by the terms 'tribe' and 'tribal
society'? What are the likely strengths and weaknesses of tribal
societies?   ▶▶

Are there any ways in which the church is like a tribal community in its thinking and practice? Is this a strength or a weakness or
both?

📖 **Read Matthew 28:16–20** – Jesus' final commission to his disciples. Here the twelve disciples are commissioned to make
disciples of all nations (Matthew 28:19). The twelve disciples
can therefore be seen as a parallel to the traditional twelve
tribes of Israel.

To what extent might this be seen as a move from tribalism to universalism? What theological significance do you see this as having?
What other elements are there in Christian thinking and practice
that you would use to support your views?

Is it possible to reconcile a Christian concern for universalism
with a strong sense of community? What implications does this
have for Christian thinking and practice?

Contingent communities

We have seen that community is something of a fuzzy term. It has
served both as a tool of analysis and a term of approbation in public dis-
course. The analytical fuzziness arises from the use of the term
community to refer to the (implied) social structure of a locality, a
commonality of interests, and an expression of values ('community
spirit'). These are three different phenomena. The question of the extent
to which any two or all three of them coincide is an empirical question.
Like other sociologists who have 'done community studies' I have never
assumed that there was a structure of relationships waiting to be found
or that statements about 'the community' were wholly disinterested
observations from impartial observers. I started with questions in the
back of my mind (although they always seemed such obvious questions
I may not have written them in books and articles): What kind of structures had grown up around which interests in this locality; how do they
relate to outside factors; to what extent and in what circumstances were
differences of interest within the locality overcome and a single
'community' interest truly expressed?

This recognises the existence of particular social structures in a locality as highly contingent. One expects both change and continuity. One asks about the way in which the wider world impinges upon the locality and how the locality manages the impacts. Issues of inequality between men and women in Bethnal Green are linked to debates about power and inequality in the welfare state. The black community in Newham was hammered together by a white racism that has both long and immediate historical origins at the national level and local origins in conflicts for scarce resources. The black community may be divided by the provision of resources, just as a community brought together by a disaster may be divided over the use of the fund set up to provide relief. We may all celebrate our identification with Liverpool or Manchester when they win the cup but be involved in bitter class or racial conflicts for the rest of the year. We may celebrate and identify with the hardihood and enterprise of the fishermen at the other end of town when talking to people outside the town, but despise their culture and ridicule their attitudes in discussions with our next-door neighbours.

EXERCISE

Think about the communities to which you belong and give attention to the following questions:

- How stable are they?
- What changes have you noticed?
- What factors have strengthened or weakened these communities?
- Have these been internal or external factors?

We can all find people who believe that things have changed for the worse. Wherever we live, town or country, there was a time not long ago when we could all go out and leave our doors unlocked. People respected one another, neighbours were helpful, children were polite and everyone looked up to the policeman and the school teacher. We may nod sagely in the high street or over the garden fence but as serious students of society we have to recognise these sentiments as statements requiring research, not simple affirmation.

Crow and Allan (1994) are supporters of the community studies tradition but they raise the interesting question of the extent to which we may be misled by the idea of community. Perhaps we should recognise the strength of this point. All act within complex and over-lapping networks of social relations based on family, work and locality. When we seek to understand social relations in a locality we should not start from the idea of community but of networks. When we understand the networks we may be able to answer such questions as: Do networks and interests overlap sufficiently for us to say there is a community here? What are the particular contingencies that could create or disrupt these networks so as to make or unmake a community? The closer the economic and affective interests of people in an area the more likely there is to be a community. But the interests will be cross-cut by considerations of class, gender and, perhaps, 'race'.

Communities therefore do not exist, they are constantly being forged and disrupted by factors internal and external to their social or geographical location. Expressions of the spirit of the community may conceal and reinforce conflicts of interest, or they may represent a temporary transcending of the differences. The nature of communities is not given once and for all, but presents a constantly evolving variety of problems for research.

In the final analysis, Christians are not simply interested in community as something that can be neatly analysed or described. The church's mission is to reflect, embody and restore community. Christian faith is trinitarian. At the very heart of the Godhead there is a community of love: Father, Son and Holy Spirit; Creator, Redeemer and Sanctifier. If God is, by very nature, characterised by community, it is not surprising that human beings, made in God's image, themselves crave community. But, in a distorted world which falls short of God's purposes, community often seems beyond reach. The church is called to be a herald and microcosm of restored human community. When the church lives up to its calling and truly displays Christian *koinonia*, then it is modelling true community, inclusivity and wholeness. It is also demonstrating in its own life God's reconciling purposes for the world. Community is, therefore, not merely another context for the church's ministry and mission; it is its primary context which should infect all other contexts.

Further reading

Crow, G and Allan, G (1994), *Community Life: an introduction to local social relations*, London, Harvester Wheatsheaf.

Frankenberg, R (1969), *Communities in Britain: social life in town and country*, Harmondsworth, Penguin.

5. GOD'S SACRED PLACE?

Introduction

In this chapter we shall:
- identify some of the macro-level factors shaping the context for urban ministry;
- explore the impact of 'anti-urban' traditions;
- discuss some biblical paradigms of the city as 'God's sacred place' (a phrase used by Harold J Recinos (1992) in his book *Jesus Weeps: global encounters on our doorstep*);
- offer a new framework for urban mission.

Reflecting on experience

What images and experiences does the word 'city' suggest to you?

What are the things that might excite and/or concern you about the prospect of moving to live in an unknown city?

The urban reality

At the beginning of the twentieth century the vast majority of the world's population of 1.63 billion lived on the land and produced food. As the century comes to an end, by contrast, more than half of the world's 6 billion inhabitants live in towns and cities. This phenomenon began early in Great Britain. Already by 1900 it was the only major country in which less than half of the population was engaged in agriculture and as 2000 approaches 80 per cent of the population live in towns or cities of 20,000 people or more.

Urbanisation, this vast internal migration from rural to urban settings, has clearly had a dramatic impact. In recent decades, moreover, its effect has been compounded by a second phenomenon: an unparalleled pattern of global migration between nation-states. As a result, not only are urban communities bigger than ever before but they contain a racial and cultural diversity on a scale never seen before. Inevitably, these major shifts in population patterns have helped to shape the lives and concerns of individuals, as well as of communities and institutions, among them the churches.

The close proximity of urban living has eroded many physical and symbolic boundaries and exposed the inter-relatedness of private, communal and public life. The density and variety of population raises questions of personal identity and well-being, but also focuses fundamental issues of social and economic disparity and reveals the realities of public policy and institutional performance.

Contemporary towns and cities are crucibles in which traditional values are being reworked and future patterns of human community are being shaped. They can be places of celebration and energy as well as of deprivation and despair, testimonies to human generosity and inventiveness, as well as to cruelty and indifference. While the uprooting involved in both internal and global migrations enables new forms to emerge it also makes great demands on human adaptability and tolerance. For urban communities to thrive, basic human needs must be met and key issues addressed, tasks which represent a constant challenge to public resources, policies and institutions.

Some key issues

The economic base

The city has always provided the public context for wide-ranging human activity: education, leisure, commerce, culture. Indeed, in an evocative image Lewis Mumford, an influential historian of cities and urban planning, refers to the city as the 'theatre', the arena in which diverse forms of human endeavour are brought together and interact:

> The city in its complete sense, then, is a geographic plexus, an economic organization, an institutional process, a theatre of social action and an aesthetic symbol of collective unity. It is in the city, the city as theatre, that man's more purposive activities are focused and worked out, through conflicting and cooperating personalities, events, groups, into more significant culminations (Mumford, 1996).

Nonetheless, the shape and sustainability of the city have always depended on its economic base, and at different stages of urban development economic forces have left their mark. The medieval walled city, for example, not only protected from marauders and rivals but also speaks of a closely knit commercial unit within which craftspeople and traders gathered round the central and symbolic market square. The sprawling towns and cities of the industrial revolution, by contrast, were enabled by the far greater economic productivity of the factory system which both sustained the dense populations and, in turn, required local pools of labour.

Equally, for the individuals involved, the quality of urban experience has always depended on the extent of their access to economic resources, and thereby to the wider life of the community. Nowhere are the world's dramatic disparities of wealth, power and lifestyle as apparent as in the visible contrasts between individuals or communities which are juxtaposed within the urban arena.

Within British cities the social and economic profile no longer resembles a pyramid with few at the top and many at the bottom. Instead it has been compared with a spinning top with narrow apex and base and bulging middle (The Methodist Church and NCH Action for Children, 1997, p. 102). At the same time there is increasing evidence of a new and worrying reality: while the simple polarity between rich and poor may have been modified, an increasing gap is emerging between those with *average* resources and the poor.

That phenomenon reflects in part the impact of two far-reaching trends: the globalisation of capital and the revolution in information technology. In order to cut labour costs and escape more restrictive legislation, many jobs in manufacturing industries have been withdrawn from Britain and relocated in places where labour and production costs are cheaper, the five-year period 1971 to 1976 alone witnessing a loss of 30 per cent of manufacturing jobs (Lawless, 1989, p. 4). The impact of this corporate restructuring on urban areas is starkly demonstrated by Lawless (1989, p. 29) who records that between 1960 and 1981 London lost 51 per cent of its manufacturing jobs and other major conurbations lost 43 per cent, while small towns lost only 1 per cent and rural areas gained 24 per cent. This process has been facilitated by the revolution in information technology which enables and supports new patterns of work which transcend the constraints of physical location. At the same time those new possibilities require, and have generated, new service industries: teams of technical, legal, financial, training or design specialists. This double effect has shifted the balance in jobs away from the low-skilled to the highly skilled, with the result that fewer people earn more money.

These international trends have been further reinforced by a series of national economic policies implemented since the early 80s in order 'to reduce public expenditure, to liberate enterprise and to eradicate inflation, combined with a determination to limit local government spending and intervention' (Lawless, 1989, p. 15). They have, moreover, been linked to a number of political initiatives designed to control public sector influence, including the abolition of the Metropolitan Counties, including the Greater London Council, in 1986, and the reduction of public housing stock in the wake of the 1988 Housing Act.

The net result of these policies has been to undermine local government agencies and strategic planning and to withdraw significant resources, particularly from those urban areas in which public services are so crucial.

The spatial dimension

This process has contributed to the historic regional differences within Britain, since the movement of employment and investment has been away from the heavy industry and manufacturing areas of the North and Midlands and towards the commercial and service jobs of the South-East. It also has a spatial dimension within given cities, for while well-paid employment creates choices of location and lifestyle, those denied such resources are radically restricted in their choice. As a consequence, socially excluded individuals find themselves predominantly in multi-disadvantaged localities.

This pattern is part of a larger demographic phenomenon within recent decades which began with a decline in the population levels of many urban centres. In his survey of the period, Lawless (1989, pp. 21f) notes that between 1971 and 1981 eight principal cities lost 1 per cent of their population each year while between 1981 and 1985 the rate of loss had reduced to 0.33 per cent. Within that same period Glasgow, Manchester and Liverpool lost 15 per cent of their total populations while some inner London boroughs suffered a decline of up to 25 per cent. This was mainly the result of a planned process of dispersal through the creation of 28 new towns between 1946 and 1987 housing a total of 1.1 million people. This programme was in part intended to alleviate the concentration of problems within inner urban areas but seems to have had the opposite effect. The evidence is that those who were most socially mobile were in the best position to take advantage of the opportunity to relocate to areas which offered cheaper housing in more environmentally friendly areas.

As a result, disproportionate numbers of the most vulnerable were left behind in pockets of the inner city or on outer estates, among them the unemployed, single-parent families, the very old and the very young. Although demographic trends now indicate renewed population growth in inner urban areas, this increase has tended merely to exacerbate the levels of multiple deprivation which are characteristic of such areas.

In addition to the intense practical pressures in areas of inadequate community resources – often exacerbated for example by the withdrawal of shops, post offices and banks or the exclusion of whole areas for credit purposes – residents of the inner city or estates are often made the scapegoats for the problems of which they are so often the victims.

This 'culture of poverty' thesis attributes a cycle of anti-social behaviour to attitudes sustained and transmitted by groups and families located in certain areas. Such a view is clearly politically expedient, since it enables the blame for complex urban problems to be focused on the inadequacy of individuals rather than on underlying structural factors. Despite research findings to the contrary, the thesis continues to attract its supporters and has re-emerged in debates about the 'deserving' and 'undeserving' poor or, more recently still about the existence of an 'underclass' (see the account by Russell, 1995, pp. 65ff).

EXERCISE
Why is it so much easier to blame individuals for their own problems rather than examine whether there are any other underlying causes?

Structural factors in social exclusion
In the first half of the 1980s a series of urban disturbances throughout the United Kingdom reflected the extent of political alienation felt by many young single men in the cities. Some of these were racial confrontations, not least the reaction of black youngsters against heavy policing tactics, but by no means all. More informed commentators identified the underlying causes in the economic, physical and social environments of many older urban areas.

Out of its own concern for the deteriorating situation in many urban priority areas, in 1983 a Church of England commission began to draw on its unparalleled access to the experience of local people in compiling its influential report, *Faith in the City* (The Archbishop of Canterbury's Commission on Urban Priority Areas, 1985). The report ranges widely in its attempt to influence the future shape of the urban church but also future urban policy, including poverty, employment and work; housing; health; social care and community work; education and young people; order and law.

That same concern has also led to the more recent Methodist report, *The Cities*. This report testifies to the fact that all of the structural problems identified in *Faith in the City* remain to be addressed. Reflecting a greater environmental awareness, it also draws attention to key issues in the search for urban sustainability: pollution, traffic, waste, energy, urban design and green spaces (The Methodist Church and NCH Action for Children, 1987, pp. 142ff). In a brief but significant section the report also focuses on the factors that reinforce and compound the experience of social exclusion. Drawing on recent research, four such factors in particular are identified: housing allocation, the labour market, poverty and low income, and racism. Since these factors have such far-reaching effects the report's findings on each point are summarised here (for a full account see The Methodist Church and NCH Action for Children, 1987, pp. 103–116).

Housing
Poorer housing conditions in disadvantaged urban areas have a number of interrelated causes. The extensive building schemes of the 1960s and 1970s often created hostile environments and, thirty or so years on, now require extensive modernisation, if not replacement. This is significant in areas which depend to a great extent on public housing and is a situation which was exacerbated by the 'Right to Buy' policy of the 1980s which led to the best of the public sector stock in the more desirable locations being sold. Meanwhile there is often inadequate public funding available to maintain poorer quality and less desirable stock. This illustrates how the right to choose not only invariably benefits the socially mobile but also prejudices those who are trapped in their location.

The situation is not greatly improved with regard to owner-occupiers. Compared with most other areas there are fewer home-owners in disadvantaged urban communities and, while more affluent home-owners may have moved away, others, including many older owner-occupiers, are unable to move out but at the same time have difficulty maintaining their homes in good repair.

The public housing that is available, moreover, is increasingly required by poor households, including homeless applicants, many of whom are dependent on welfare benefits, and those made unemployed by the economic restructuring of the cities. As a corollary, middle-income families are deterred from applying for public housing since rent levels have been fuelled by patterns of housing benefit subsidy: those on housing benefit have the rent increases paid while others find the rents increasingly uneconomical. This pattern serves only to reinforce the link between public-sector housing and low-income tenants.

Employment

Difficulties in the urban employment market vary greatly according to location. Where estates were designed to house the workforce for a major local employer there is a particular risk of vulnerability should that source of employment fail. The search for alternative work is also likely to be made more difficult by the physical isolation of the estates and the frequent inadequacy of public transport.

Work within inner-city areas is often restricted to 'low paid, insecure employment, possibly part-time and with poor promotion prospects' (The Methodist Church and NCH Action for Children, 1987, p. 109). In addition, those seeking work from inner-city areas have to compete in large labour markets which are advertised to, and easily accessed from, the city as a whole. From such a base it is often difficult to establish long-term and relevant work experience, which is often the prerequisite of more secure jobs, or to become part of those informal working networks through which information about vacancies is shared.

Poverty and low income

Despite the absence of a universally accepted definition of poverty in Britain, official statistics indicate that those groups acknowledged to have the lowest disposable income, or most likely to be on means-tested benefits, are pensioners, the unemployed, those on low incomes, single-parent families, the sick and disabled. All are present in significant numbers in inner-city areas.

Areas of high unemployment and low income also experience further disadvantage. The lack of purchasing power leads to a reduced demand for local goods and services, with clear knock-on effects for local businesses and provisions. Poverty affects diet and lifestyle and there is clear evidence that inequalities in health and life expectancy mirror inequalities in wealth. Inadequate levels of income have led to an extensive problem of debt, a problem that has been dramatically symbolised in many areas by the re-appearance of pawnbrokers.

Racism

Britain's black population lives primarily in London and in the towns and cities of the Midlands and North-West. Within those regions, moreover, they are often concentrated in the most disadvantaged neighbourhoods due to the combination of discriminatory practices in the housing and labour markets.

While the free market at work within the privately rented sector may encourage discriminatory practices, there are also problems within the regulated public sector. Ethnic minority families who have recently arrived in Britain are disadvantaged by a points system that favours those who have been on the list a long time or have long-established links with an area. They are, moreover, often housed under homelessness legislation that tends to channel applicants towards lower-quality accommodation.

Employment practices are also suspect, with Afro-Caribbean and Asian young people experiencing significantly higher rates of unemployment, two and three times as high respectively, than their white counterparts of the same age and qualifications. There is evidence that both direct and indirect racism are at work in shaping employers' expectations of 'suitable' applicants and in their choice of information and recruitment channels.

Since *The Cities* report, issues of racism have been focused in a particularly poignant way by the 1999 report into the murder of the black teenager Stephen Lawrence. Its public indictment of the institutionalised racism found within the Metropolitan Police has been heralded as a watershed in challenging the structural, as well as individual, manifestations of the problem.

The consequences of any of these four factors are often very costly in human terms. Their combined effect can clearly be devastating for whole communities: as those who are socially least mobile, and economically most vulnerable, are concentrated in areas which often contain the worst conditions of housing, unemployment, low income and inadequate services.

> **EXERCISE**
> What are the main issues for people living in your neighbourhood?
>
> Are they similar or very different from the issues outlined above?

A bifocal vision

Despite these factors, and the cycles of deprivation to which they so easily lead, it would be wrong to see the city only in negative terms: as a source of problems on a scale which warrants apocalyptic imagery of 'crisis' or 'doom'. Such a view might well draw on and contribute to the long-established anti-urban tradition with its tendency to see cities as centres of vice and evil (see the discussion in Leech, 1988, pp. 25f). It may further reflect nostalgia for an idealised rural existence to which the British are particularly prone. It may also provide the mythology that helps rationalise and justify the flight away from the city to the suburbs, which has a long history.

But it offers at best a partial account of urban reality. It overlooks the resilience, energy, inventiveness and courage of many individuals and their families. It ignores the commitment and human investment of many community groups and networks. It discounts the wealth of cultural diversity that is evident in so many places and guises. Alongside the structural problems that undoubtedly exist there is also enormous potential and creativity to explore.

An adequate awareness of the city must embrace this bifocal vision. For the Christian community a powerful resource in establishing that awareness is the rediscovery of a number of biblical paradigms which evoke both positive and challenging images of the city as a place of revelation and discovery, as 'God's sacred space'.

God's sacred place: a biblical perspective

The holy city

Central to Jewish scriptural tradition is Zion, the holy city, the place where God is truly worshipped (see, for instance, Psalm 99). This is the place where God brings hope, where justice is proclaimed and where God's people claim their identity. While, according to the accounts of Genesis, human origins are located in the Garden of Eden, the biblical canon locates its vision of the fulfilment and perfection of the created order in the Holy City, the heavenly Jerusalem, of the Book of Revelation. This is envisioned as the place of God's enduring presence with the human family. It is to be a model city of faith and morality, one where 'abomination and falsehood' are eliminated and 'every tear wiped dry' (Revelation 21:4, 8). It is true that the historical city of Jerusalem is sometimes subjected to severe criticism in the Bible, not least by some of the prophets (for example, Amos 6:1) and by Jesus (for example, Matthew 23:37), but this by no means reflects an anti-urban bias; rather it underlines the central symbolic importance of the holy city, Zion.

The city as a place of shalom

The Hebrew biblical tradition insists that a basic requirement of the authentic faith community is *shalom*, a word with no simple English equivalent. It certainly includes the notion of 'peace', by which it is often translated, but embraces a much wider sense of that well-being which can only result from all basic human needs – economic, political, social and spiritual – being met. As a result it implies health, security, prosperity, unity with nature and a heightened spirituality. True *shalom* cannot be experienced by an individual alone, since its attainment implies a community dimension. As a holistic biblical concept, the notion of *shalom* offers an important corrective to simplistic readings of urban reality that are too easily promoted by the popular media or political processes.

EXERCISE

📖 **Read Jeremiah 29:4–9** – Jeremiah's advice to the community of exiles in Babylon.

What might it mean for communities of faith to 'seek the *shalom* of the city' today?

The global city

A further perspective is provided by the account of the church on the day of Pentecost in Acts 2. As the Spirit was poured on the disciples and the people of Jerusalem a common understanding was experienced, despite the presence of different languages and the racial and cultural differences that they represented. The possibility and enrichment of communication across cultures and traditions is here described as a gift of the Spirit. In many urban contexts the church has a God-given opportunity to become a laboratory of the Spirit in the search for new forms of community that need to be modelled for the wider society. The Pentecost experience is a parable of what it might mean for Christians to celebrate the riches and opportunities of the multi-cultural community, rather than being negative or wary about it.

The city of surprises

EXERCISE
📖 **Read Matthew 25:31–45.**

What attitudes towards the city and its residents might it be appropriate for the church to adopt in the light of such a passage?

Jesus' parable of the Good Samaritan in Luke 10:25–37 offers new resonances for the church in the urban context. The church's vocation to become the neighbour to the vulnerable, to the victim, and to those robbed of dignity or opportunity is clearly understood if not always effectively embodied. The extra, critical dimension of the parable is that it is the Samaritan, the one who is marginalised, discriminated against and powerless in the dominant society, who here becomes the bearer of God's word, the one who is chosen to bring the good news to the church. As in the parable of the Last Judgement (Matthew 25:31–45) the least and the least likely can prove to be surprising channels of grace. Similarly, the urban context and experience are major opportunities to be grasped, if churches will allow themselves to be invited or provoked into new discoveries about their communities and new revelations about their God.

A new framework for urban mission

The church has rarely been effective in urban settings. While there may be a variety of contributing factors to this failure, it is based in part on a loss of the bifocal vision which has led to a collusion with those tendencies which emphasise the negative aspects of urban communities. As a consequence it has adopted a variety of unhelpful strategies: withdrawal from the city, the maintenance of spiritual ghettos within the city or, at best, mission to the city by seeking to solve its problems. The task of the urban church today is, however, in process of redefinition, reflecting both a re-reading of the biblical tradition and also a sensitivity to a range of contemporary factors.

EXERCISE

What images do you find most helpful in thinking about the mission of the church?

Do they suggest a one-way process of 'going, giving, proclaiming' or do they allow that the church might also learn and receive?

The thrust of the biblical paradigms is to invite the church to view the city as the arena for human renewal and redemption. This is where individual tears are to be wiped dry, holistic understandings of life explored and new communities formed as acted parables of God's Kingdom. Such paradigms require an understanding of the church as an agent of God's grace and presence, proclaiming and anticipating a fulfilment of individual and corporate experience which is consistently denied by so much contemporary experience. As such, it is called to be an agent of transformation working for the renewal of the city, not merely a gathering of the worshipping people within it.

Such an understanding invites new commitments: a willingness to be alongside and to listen to the experience of urban communities; a recognition of the need to receive and learn from their wealth of human and spiritual resources, as well as to give. In this process the framework of ministry is likely to be recast. The challenge is to develop forms of Christian presence, worship and engagement which are authentic to the complex, multi-dimensional communities which characterise contemporary urban life.

Further reading

Bradbury, N (1989), *City of God? pastoral care in the inner city*, London, SPCK.
Cathcart, B (1999), *The Case of Stephen Lawrence*, London, Viking.
Meyers, E S (ed.) (1992), *Envisioning the New City: a reader on urban ministry*, Louisville, Kentucky, Westminster John Knox Press.

Northcott, M (ed.) (1998), *Urban Theology: a reader*, London, Cassell.

Rowland, C and Vincent, J (eds) (1997), *Gospel from the City*, Sheffield, Urban Theology Unit.

Rogers, R (1997), *Cities for a Small Planet*, London, Faber and Faber.

Sedgwick, P (ed.) (1995), *God in the City*, London, Mowbray.

6. POOR AND POWERLESS?

Introduction

In this chapter we shall:
- analyse some of the contextual factors which shape urban local congregational life;
- evaluate some models of engagement with the wider urban community;
- identify recurrent themes in Christian responses to the urban context.

The previous chapter identifies some of the factors which shape the contemporary context for urban ministry at a macro level. In this chapter the focus of attention now turns to the more local level: if urban churches are to take their context seriously they need to work at what it means to be the church in their particular place. That context not only helps to define the nature and self-understanding of the congregation, but also highlights the need for the church to find ways to engage with the wider urban issues. In that process a number of key issues emerge which constitute challenges to the church, but also offer real opportunities for it to contribute to the well-being of the city.

Reflecting on experience
What do you think could be the main benefits of belonging to a multi-racial congregation?

What could the experience of a multi-racial congregation contribute to the wider community?

The urban congregation

The range of factors which mould the wider urban context have inevitably implications for local urban congregations, and models of church life developed in other contexts are often inappropriate and cannot simply be imported. Urban situations themselves of course vary greatly between, for example, traditional industrial towns, outer estates and metropolitan conurbations. Individual congregations, moreover, each have their own distinct identity and some may exhibit few of the common characteristics. Nonetheless the following features often play a significant role in shaping the profile of many urban congregations, especially in inner-city areas.

A multi-racial dimension

Typically the inner-city congregation reflects the wider multi-racial mix of the city. In many situations, indeed, church life has been renewed and transformed by patterns of immigration which have brought Christians from all over the world to repopulate British churches which until then were in a process of decline. Over the last thirty years in particular significant numbers of church members have arrived from the West Indies and, more recently, West Africa. Many tell of their initial disillusion on arriving only to discover that their image of the United Kingdom as a Christian country was quickly shattered both by the state of the churches and, far too often, by the racial prejudice of white church members who were less than welcoming. Some stayed within the mainstream denominations that were familiar from home. Others left to join independent black churches which remain an important feature of the urban church scene. As a result of this process many inner-city congregations include a wide range of cultural backgrounds.

Within that cultural variety there are also very diverse experiences and expectations of church and ministry which need to be recognised and negotiated. Often there is a high regard for sacramental ministry, even with the Free Churches where the sacraments have traditionally received less emphasis. There are often extensive supportive pastoral networks of families and friends which emerge and become very evident in the major family events of baptisms, weddings, funerals or memorial services. Different liturgical ceremonies may be requested as important events or traditions become the focus for community celebrations. Such occasions clearly require the local church to be open to a range of cultural needs and sensitivities, but the opportunities for learning and sharing are enormous. The contribution of the church in enabling such cultural traditions to be expressed is vital. This is increasingly so as second and third generation members of the different communities try to sustain something of their cultural heritage.

A major issue for the future demography of many traditional urban congregations is the extent to which British-born black youngsters will replicate the patterns of church attendance of their parents or grandparents. If they were either to share the disaffection from church allegiance of their white peers or, alternatively, support the independent black churches which currently show signs of growth, the impact on the mainstream denominations could be quite dramatic.

People on the move

While many urban congregations will have a small core of regular and often elderly attenders, the group as a whole often has a high turnover of membership, due to the large number of people in transit for one reason or another. Some may be in temporary accommodation awaiting re-housing by the council. Others may come to the city on short-term contracts or courses. Yet others will move out of the inner-urban area in search of better housing or schooling. Recent arrivals to the UK will often stay with family members until establishing their own home and then move on. Some who have settled in the UK from other countries may periodically travel home for extended periods or return home in retirement.

Even those who rarely if ever move home may be able to sustain only spasmodic involvement in a local church. This is often due to a variety of practical pressures to which many are subject: for example, irregular or multiple part-time jobs; shift work; problems with transport or child care; or membership of cultural networks or extended families which have their own expectations or demands.

As a consequence of these different factors traditions are often short-lived in the local church. There may be a continual sense of having to start from the beginning and a difficulty in sustaining longer-term developments. Those who may be in a position to offer local leadership are often hard to find or retain. Continuity of programmes or pastoral contacts may be difficult. Spontaneity rather than order is likely to prevail and the keeping of accurate records remains a recurrent challenge!

A sense of vulnerability

The urban congregation encounters vulnerability at different levels. Some of its regular members are themselves very vulnerable people: socially, economically, emotionally. Sometimes the congregation is small or predominantly elderly. There may be uncertainty about the future, especially if there are no financial reserves, or the building is a liability, or there is doubt whether the current paid staff will be replaced.

Those who come onto the premises or into the services may also introduce vulnerability. Among the pressures of urban living the churches still suggest places of refuge, tolerance and caring for those who walk in off the streets or ring the doorbell for advice or help. In their attempts to be welcoming and available congregations sometimes have to make themselves vulnerable, while church buildings too can become ready targets of vandalism or break-ins. The conflicting demands of accessibility and security have always to be reconciled.

EXERCISE
📖 Read 1 Corinthians 1:25–31.

How far is vulnerability a proper mark of the Christian community?

Yet again the sheer invisibility of many churches within the complex urban environment is a real factor: in addition to being surrounded and overshadowed by high-rise offices, flats and civic buildings, congregations are also often confronted by a population density and a scale of human need which may lead them to question their own sense of significance. Arguably, however, that very sense of vulnerability is an important source of strength. It helps local congregations to empathise and share solidarity with their vulnerable neighbours. It dispels any illusions that any local church can, or should, seek solutions to the needs of urban people without consultation, alliances or partnerships. It underlines the vocation of the Christian community, which is called to live by grace.

Building up the common life

The task of building up the common life is one to which most churches would subscribe. Among diverse, mobile and vulnerable congregations, however, it warrants the highest priority. The creation of a church community which welcomes and affirms a variety of people, many of whom have known isolation or marginalisation, makes a powerful theological statement about the inclusive love of God. The social experience of belonging and participating in such a community offers many a unique source of support, solidarity and confidence.

While this community building can be furthered by all that the church attempts, it is often focused by the occasions of public worship, which may be the only time that the congregation gathers together to any significant degree. As a result, whatever the liturgical traditions of different churches, a common feature is often the attempt to encourage inclusion and participation. This may itself represent a particular challenge to the creative imagination when the congregation consists of many who do not share a 'book culture' or for whom English may be a second or third language. Sometimes elements of the liturgy are opened up by inviting people to share their concerns for prayer or by dialogical sermons. At other times the non-liturgical elements of worship are developed: the notices slot is extended into a sharing of community events and news, welcomes and farewells: the recognition of significant personal events to which many have an opportunity to contribute. Not infrequently, congregational discussions or decision-making meetings or shared meals may be associated with the worship, or be incorporated within it, since this may be the only time a significant group of the community gathers together. In a variety of ways liturgy re-establishes its original, broader meaning as 'an act of public service'.

Promoting community

The Church of England's *Faith in the City* report (Archbishop of Canterbury's Commission on Urban Priority Areas, 1985, p. 57) recognised that:

> The working of economic and social processes depends ultimately upon securing the willing co-operation of people. It is the neglect of this crucial human factor which we have seen to be responsible for some of the worst social conditions in our cities today; and this has led us to ... lay great emphasis on forms of action and service which are

intermediate between personal ministry to individuals and political action directed towards society as a whole. These are forms of action which promote community.

This judgement of the *Faith in the City* report – which is also a continued emphasis in the Methodist report, *The Cities* (The Methodist Church and NCH Action for Children, 1997) a decade later – focuses an important task for the urban church beyond its proper attention to the immediate pastoral and spiritual needs of the local congregation. Not that this is ultimately a different task, since church members are members of the wider community: its *shalom* and theirs are inextricably bound together. Similarly it is precisely as a constituent part of the local neighbourhood, not as a separate agency, that the church can help to promote community.

EXERCISE
Do you agree that one task of the church is to 'promote community'?

How do you think that fits in with other tasks of the church?

At one level the very presence of a church and the myriad activities of its individual members, as parents, neighbours, home-helps, members of tenants' associations, etc., can have a significant humanising effect. Nonetheless, the emphasis here is on the more conscious and focused contributions of the church as an organisation. The routes which different churches follow will vary greatly and will often be determined by local opportunities and needs, as well as by the skills and convictions of any single congregation. There are, however, a number of distinctive models which have been widely adopted.

Networking
The task of involving people in the rebuilding of their communities is one which requires the widest possible collaboration of local individuals, the voluntary sector and statutory agencies. The aim is to share experience and expertise, to ensure more effective analysis and action. The initial and often most productive means is networking: establishing and maintaining contacts, identifying local leaders,

drawing people together around common issues or concerns, making links across the natural, social or professional groupings.

Most urban practitioners cultivate their networks, as do local residents. The church is often in a particularly good position to play a role in community networking due to a number of factors. Large or small, it represents a group of mainly local people who are committed to embody community, sometimes across those very barriers of age or race which otherwise can divide, and as such it can draw together a wide range of experience and knowledge. It has contacts in, and an unparalleled access to, many different sectors of the community. Its buildings offer space for a range of community groups, meetings or events and can be useful as 'neutral territory' where many different interests might meet. Despite any apparent apathy towards formal religious activity, the church is often recognised to have a long-term commitment to the neighbourhood and is still associated with such virtues as integrity and compassion which enable it to play an important role as 'honest broker' in many situations. These factors are real and significant. They represent a trust which must be honoured, but also an opportunity to share in the process of networking which itself can lead to involvement in wide-ranging community activities.

Projects

Many urban churches try to express their concern for the community in specific practical projects. The scale of those projects varies enormously from the handful of volunteers serving refreshments at the weekly 'drop-in' to highly professional full-time staff running permanent residential accommodation. The range of services is also very broad, with many examples of established projects in day centres and night-shelters, lunch clubs and advice work, support groups, therapeutic groups and rehabilitation centres, training courses, youth clubs and the like. The responsiveness of many congregations is also reflected, moreover, in the development of new styles of work to meet new needs: for instance, supplementary education and homework clubs, credit unions and debt advice, contact centres and non-alcoholic bars. Such projects often represent a valuable community facility as well as a legitimate expression of Christian compassion. They are often very accessible to local people, due to their humane scale and informal style as well as their location in the immediate neighbourhood.

> **EXERCISE**
> Have you ever been part of a church which genuinely tried to engage with its local community? What do you think were its motives? What did it achieve?

Church projects, however, increasingly have to cope with a range of management issues, not least as they develop, employ staff and become dependent on external funding. Securing the funding itself takes a great deal of time and is becoming more and more competitive. The responsibilities of management committees have expanded as employers and as those charged with implementing a range of statutory requirements and procedures. The contemporary 'contract culture' demands precise targets and outcomes for agreed services both in terms of quantity and quality.

As the service offered becomes more professional it may also be harder to sustain the church's support and ownership of the work. Certainly expectations need to be clarified and the commitments of time, energy and resources negotiated. At the same time such projects present significant opportunities for the church to be involved creatively in the local community and to share in dialogue about common values as well as practical policies. (For an excellent extended discussion of community ministry see *Beyond the Good Samaritan* by Ann Morisy, 1997.)

Regeneration

Whereas projects are normally focused on a particular service or client group, community regeneration is concerned with a more integral approach to urban development. In Bromley by Bow in East London, for example, a church centre has become an agency through which a programme integrating the 'community, arts, education, health, environment and liturgy' has been brought together and government funding for a £1.2 million health centre secured (Mawson, 1995, p. 139). While the programme itself is impressive, so is the commitment to develop the creativity and potential for growth of those who are involved (see Mawson, 1995, pp. 157–160).

Such opportunities are either created by social entrepreneurs (individuals seeking innovative and socially just solutions to community problems) or offered to selected communities by a variety of government-funded initiatives: in recent years the *City Challenge* programme, the *Single Regeneration Budget* or, most recently, *New Deal for Communities*. At best such programmes offer an integral 'joined up' approach to a range of urban issues within a particular locality. At worst they target resources, on the basis of competitive bids in which there are bound to be more losers than winners, at schemes which lack adequate local consultation. In the process, churches may themselves be able to provide elements of the services for which funding is being offered to coalitions of community groups.

Organising

The most far-reaching strategic response to the need to promote community is represented by Community, or Broad-Based, Organising, a movement which has a history of 50 years' experience in the USA where it was founded and developed by a community activist, Saul Alinsky. Within the UK it is a much more recent phenomenon with organisations emerging in half a dozen urban areas within the last decade. Organising has been defined as 'the process by which the people of an urban community organise themselves to deal with the primary forces that are exploiting their community and making them powerless victims' (Linthicum, 1992, p. 115). That definition indicates the central role of local people who are encouraged and enabled to act together to identify key community issues and to address people and issues of power. While Organising focuses on specific issues, its vision is much wider, concerned as it is to recreate the possibility and experience of individual participation in public and community issues: 'to reweave the fabric of civic society' (see Citizen Organising Foundation, 1997).

The prime facilitators of the movement in any locality are full-time trained staff. By a programme of systematic visiting and networking of individuals and groups they invite commitment, help to identify and research key issues around which coalitions are built, train local leaders and design programmes of action. Their ability to create a broad-based coalition and to give communities the experience of achieving attainable and winnable goals is impressive, though the tactics of confrontation often associated with community organising have proven inimical to some.

Broad-Based Organising, by definition and intent, is certainly not a church initiative and its very effectiveness depends on identifying the mutual interests of a wide variety of people. Faith communities of all kinds can and do, however, have an important role. They are recognised as key players in any local community as those groups that are most clearly committed to exploring human values and to seeking the wider welfare of the community.

EXERCISE
📖 **Read Luke 4:16–21.**

How far could Jesus' sermon in Nazareth serve as a 'manifesto' for the contemporary urban church?

Advocacy

As was seen in the previous chapter, local urban issues are often expressions of much wider social, economic or political policies or phenomena. In promoting community, churches may be called to share in the task of wider advocacy in order that decisions taken elsewhere may be informed by local experience and priorities.

That advocacy may be needed at a city-wide level and churches may again be well placed to take or support appropriate initiatives. It may be that an ecumenical group of church leaders, who may play a significant role within the civic context, can be briefed to raise issues publicly or with the appropriate officials. It may be that a civic forum exists of which the churches, along with other faith communities, are a part, for example, the *Human City Project* in Birmingham or the London network of Ecumenical Borough Deans. It may be that the wider church needs to understand more about urban reality in order to challenge misconceptions or shape the allocation of resources. At least such occasions might be opportunities for churches to act as the agents through which local experience can be harvested, collated and used to inform or influence others. At best they may be opportunities for the church to enable those who can testify to the experience of poverty or social exclusion to speak for themselves and be heard; *The Cities* (The Methodist Church and NCH Action for Children, 1987, p. 182) cites the examples of the 'Bradford Urban Hearings' and the Church Action on Poverty programme, 'Local People National Voice'.

Some recurrent themes

In the church's attempt to respond to the demands and opportunities of its urban setting and to contribute to the promotion of the wider community a number of themes recur:

A broadening of the pastoral agenda

The experience of urban churches makes it clear that while pastoral care includes common elements of personal support (such as in moments of crisis, illness, or bereavement) it also embraces a much wider range of issues. Problems associated with housing, immigration status, crime, welfare benefits, and debt all appear on the pastoral agenda, along with many more. Pastoral caring is not restricted to personal support but often involves engagement with other agencies or statutory bodies. Boundaries between pastoral concerns and public issues are often blurred, while short-term support can indicate the need for long-term policy change.

Hospitality

Within the New Testament the word for hospitality is *philoxenia*, meaning love or care for the stranger. Its opposite is the more familiar *xenophobia*. Within the urban context hospitality is a central part of the church's ministry and is expressed in a variety of ways. Hospitality is an aspect of an open community which welcomes the stranger, the visitor, the marginal and the different. Hospitality is expressed in making church premises available to other groups and congregations. Hospitality can be the style which encourages networking or influences how projects are run. The church also needs a willingness to accept hospitality: to receive from other traditions, cultures, agencies; to share what they have to offer and to affirm it; to encourage mutuality for the good of all.

Empowerment

While the churches have a long and honourable record of working *for* the community and its poorest or most marginalised members, the greater challenge is to learn ways of working *with* or alongside. The issue is one of empowerment, without which members of the urban community will remain dependent and voiceless. The change of culture required is unlikely to come easily or without many mistakes being made. The task of transforming the urban church community itself, however, so that it becomes a place where people are empowered and collaboration experienced, could be an excellent way to begin. Certainly, unless the church community models and reflects those intentions, it will have little credibility when it seeks to address the wider community.

EXERCISE

Can you recall a situation when you felt powerless? How did it feel?

What effect could such an experience have on a whole group or community?

Partnerships

The task of promoting community, let alone transforming structural problems, is one which requires a willingness to engage in a variety of partnerships and alliances. There is an ecumenical imperative to work as closely together as possible with other churches to seek the welfare of the city. Increasingly, that spirit of co-operation is likely to extend to include other faith communities, either out of conviction that it should or out of pragmatic necessity. The Inner Cities Religious Council has had government support for a number of years in its attempts to draw faith communities together to address issues of community regeneration. Recent government initiatives, for example the *New Deal for Communities,* will look as a matter of course for broadly based alliances within which all the faith communities have been invited to take part. At a wider level too, public funding programmes seem likely to encourage broad community coalitions, while some church-based community projects are also turning to partnerships with voluntary, public sector and private bodies to secure their futures.

Poor and powerless?

The urban context presents a tapestry of many interdependent threads. The experiences of poverty, powerlessness and social exclusion are real and, for many, determinative. A bifocal vision, however, requires that the variety of traditions and cultures, the courage and resourcefulness of individuals, and the commitment and creativity of voluntary groups are not overlooked. While often distanced, if not alienated, from the places of formal decision-making and resource allocation, the urban community is not always bereft of power. It may, however, need encouragement, training and support to own and use those opportunities to influence its own future which do exist. Urban congregations reflect various aspects of their urban environment. They also have a contribution to make, in partnership with others, towards that promotion of community which is for them a central task. To fulfil that task new models and ways of being church may need to be explored but, in the process, important lessons for the whole church might be learned.

Further reading

Bradbury, N (1989), *City of God? pastoral care in the inner city*, London, SPCK.

Cathcart, B (1999), *The Case of Stephen Lawrence*, London, Viking.

Meyers, E S (ed.) (1992), *Envisioning the New City: a reader on urban ministry*, Louisville, Kentucky, Westminster John Knox Press.

Northcott, M (ed.) (1998), *Urban Theology: a reader*, London, Cassell.

Rowland, C and Vincent, J (eds) (1997), *Gospel from the City*, Sheffield, Urban Theology Unit.

Rogers, R (1997), *Cities for a Small Planet*, London, Faber and Faber.

Sedgwick, P (ed.) (1995), *God in the City*, London, Mowbray.

7. A PLACE ON THE MOVE

Introduction

In this chapter we shall:
- explore the suburban context for ministry;
- look beneath the smooth suburban surface to discover the complex dynamics of self, church and community;
- begin to outline some of the 'prophetic messages' that arise out of the gospel, resonating with and disturbing suburbia.

Reflecting on experience
Have you ever belonged to or visited a church in suburbia? What did you notice about:
- the kind of people who made up the congregation;
- the way the church was organised and led;
- its liturgy;
- its architecture?

How did it differ from churches you know in other types of area?

(If you have little or no experience of suburban churches find someone who does and listen to their reflections.)

What is suburbia?

In his book *The Buddha of Suburbia*, Hanif Kureishi (1990) crafted the following memorable picture of suburbia: 'a dreary suburb of London of which it was said that when people drowned they saw not their lives but their double-glazing flashing before them'. It has been estimated that half the population of England lives in suburbia of one sort of another. Suburbia might be defined as simply the outlying neighbourhoods of a city, but that would tell you very little about suburbia. Suburbia is an attempt to marry together the benefits of town and country. Modern-day suburbia owes much to the development of cheap mass transport systems in the first half of the twentieth century. The building of London's Metropolitan Railway, for instance, spawned the growth of suburbs that came to be known as 'Metroland', immortalised in the writings of John Betjeman.

EXERCISE

Commuting to work often eats up a lot of the suburban resident's time. What implications might this have for suburban churches?

Suburbia was partly a response to urban over-population and environmental degradation; the 'leafy suburbs' offered people space to breathe and the prospect of an enhanced quality of life. Those who moved out to suburbia were mostly the middle class and emergent middle class. For some, suburbia was just a staging post until they became 'ex-urban' and moved to a village or small town. Although moving to suburbia may have felt like moving to the country for many of its new residents it did, in fact, represent a form of *urbanisation* as cities sprawled ever further. Suburbia, however, frequently gives rise to counter-reactions to urbanisation, such as NIMBY-ism, as residents maintain 'Not In My Back Yard!'

Does understanding suburbia matter?

It is interesting to note that sociologists, like social workers, tend to live in suburbia but often work and write about the inner city. There is an implication that suburbia is straightforward, a place where common sense prevails. Several television soap operas such as *Neighbours* or *Brookside* sum up this particular view. While the inhabitants of Ramsey Street, for example, fall out with each other and frequently have problems, they also solve their problems and relationships with fine rapidity. The solution to apparently intractable problems is a kind word, a reasoned argument, someone 'coming to their senses'. Behind the scenes is an assumption of stability, basic goodness, reasonable intelligence. Why on earth should you need to dig deeper to understand the issues involved? If Homer was only interested in the aristocracy in his *Iliad*, then the writers of *Neighbours*, like suburbia itself, are only really interested in the middle class. Though this programme is set in Australia, there is little reference to that fact. The flora and fauna could be from almost any city in any country; the connection with the larger city is fragile; national and regional issues play no part. Suburbia in fiction has been excised from its context and placed entire unto itself for our reflection. The causes and solutions to the dilemmas that the characters face are contained within the situation. It is as if all that the participants in the drama need to do is to dig a little deeper into the inherent decency of their humanity.

It is this assumption about suburbia, which is also made within suburbia, that needs to be questioned. The smooth surface belies the inner turmoil. The longing for community, for identity with a particular place, and a place within that community, does not indicate contentment but dissatisfaction. A sense of stability may well be the aim of suburbia and its image, but it is neither the motivating force nor the reality. It is longing for something that characterises both the move outwards to suburbia and the energy that maintains it. We may develop a useful rule of thumb: 'The more obsessively interested a group are with a particular issue the less confident they are about that issue.' If suburbia seems strongly drawn to notions of neighbourhood, community and identity it is because these are the very concerns that trouble it most.

A minister's personal story: part one

One minister, Andrew, told his personal story about taking up a new appointment in suburbia in the following way:

> I arrived in my new suburban appointment with some previous experience of suburbia. I made initial assumptions about the nature of the ministry in the new place based on the past. Both churches had a similar profile of professional people. Lecturers, teachers and managers parked similar cars outside a similar-sized building. There were differences that seemed superficial and I did not let them divert me from my plan of campaign. My observations about the structure of the church, as in the previous appointment, were that we needed to develop collaborative ministry. The minister's role was hopelessly crucial to church activity. The presbyteral ministry was perceived by church members as the fountain of all blessing, but I perceived it to be the bot-

tle neck. I sought to enable a wider franchise of ministry within the church and release the considerable abilities of the congregation. We came close to disaster. The difficulties may have been exasperated by many personal factors and local issues. For example, previous ministry within this church had been exceptionally successful in pursuing hierarchical management structures. It is my opinion, however, that my fundamental error was one of simply misconstruing the situation. The surface was similar but beneath that surface there was a turbulence that swept my ministry off course. Taking notice of the answer to a simple question would have altered my understanding of what was going on: 'Where do your parents live?' The answer revealed a crucial difference. In the new appointment many of the middle class congregation had moved away from strongly working-class roots. Their parents lived nearby geographically but a further distance away socially. In the previous appointment the congregation had moved only a little distance socially, though for some many miles geographically.

The emerging middle class

Some of the problems experienced by that minister were due to his slowness to understand his congregation's different attitude to authority figures. The different attitudes of the emerging middle class, compared with the established middle class, have been well documented by sociologists. For example, in the emerging middle class there is distinct ambivalence towards authority. This ambivalence may be expressed in a strong respect for professional people that contains an antipathy and resentment. The resentment and respect originate in earlier experiences and models of community. The role of the doctor, priest, teacher or social worker in a council housing estate is one of some power and privilege. Such professionals would tend not to live on these estates but commute in. They thus both identify with and reject the community, and such a mixture occasions ambivalent reactions. A resident moving from the estate into nearby suburbia is moving next door to these professionals. While they themselves now enjoy the privilege and the power of such authority figures, they carry the memories and response patterns of their previous community. Such ambivalence lies behind the difficulties of introducing collaborative ministry styles. The authority figure is the one expected to do and decide. This is both welcomed and resented. It is welcomed because it is easy, safe and comfortable; it preserves the status quo long remembered. It is resented because the status quo has changed and the authority figure has no right to dominate.

EXERCISE

Trace your own family's social movement during this century.

- How has your family moved over the last century?
- What opportunities for education did your parents or grand-parents have?
- What jobs did they do?
- Where did they live?
- How are the next generation different?

How might this affect your view of the church and its ministry?

The complexity of life

In his book *The Social Reality of Religion*, Peter Berger (1969, p. 3) wrote as follows:

> Society is a product of man. It has no other being except that which is bestowed upon it by human activity and consciousness. There can be no social reality apart from man. Yet it may also be stated that man is a product of society. Every individual biography is an episode within the history of society, which both precedes and survives it. Society was there before the individual was born and it will be there after he has died. What is more, it is within society, and as a result of social processes, that the individual becomes a person, that he attains and holds onto an identity, and that he carries out the various projects that constitute his life.

The suburban dream and the common assumption about suburbia (its stability, independence from elsewhere and contentment) is mis-placed. We cannot abstract suburbia, however much it wants to be, from either the past or its present location. Social analysis is not an optional extra for those who would exercise ministry, it is an essential tool for understanding where you are. For suburbia is not simply complex because of where it is placed, but also because of what it is within itself. The turbulence that lies beneath the surface is not simply the con-sequence of the less tranquil waters higher up stream, but also a product of the complexity of its present position. This complexity can be expressed through the following four points:

- reality, however stable and objective it appears, is in fact the product of an inherently unstable and dynamic process;

- society is a complex product of human creativity that has an impact on humanity;
- who we are not only shapes the society in which we live but also is determined to some extent by that society;
- suburbia, complex because of where it comes from and for what it is itself, demands careful analysis if effective ministry is to occur.

What is suburbia?

It is easier to understand suburbia for what it is not, or how it has come about, than to define what it is in itself. It is not inner city, nor is it a rural community. Suburbia, despite that calm exterior, is in fact a place on the move. It is thus not a content place but a place of unease and discontent; because of this dynamic it is not *one* thing but a number of different things. One patch of suburbia may be significantly different from the next patch of suburbia only a mile or so away. For example, the minister who told his personal story earlier in this chapter was working in a patch of suburbia that contained a large number of emerging middle-class families. In such an area you would expect to find people on the move, trying to shake off their working-class roots. In other neighbouring patches of suburbia you would find that the middle class have already emerged and moved on from other suburban areas. They also may be on the move, but perhaps away from suburbia altogether, into their idea of a rural idyll – 'ex-urbia'. In the 'emerging middle class' patch of suburbia you might find people who are reluctant to shop in the market located in the working-class area from which many of them have emerged; nearby in the other suburbia, families are confident enough to shop wherever they wish. Similarly, in one suburban patch relationship to authority is profoundly ambivalent; nearby the ambivalence has been resolved to a greater degree.

A minister's personal story: part two
Andrew continued his personal story about taking up a new appointment in suburbia in the following way:

> The local residents call the community in which they live 'the village'. In this one description you have an insight into so much of the hopes and unhappiness that hold them together. Few people, if any, of those who now dwell here, have ever lived in a village. This community, under the flight path of a major international airport, comprising

road after road of post-1950s housing, is far from being the conventional idea of a rural village. It has very little community life, little local employment, and all the trappings of individualistic suburban life. During the working day only the schools offer much evidence of activity. It is, however, closer to being a village than the areas many have come from, for the parents of many still live on vast housing estates, or in inner-city terraces, and look to this place as offering rural peace.

The ideal village

For many 'the village' is a name for where they want to be: moving outwards, seeking identity, longing for community, for ownership and possession. In suburbia the Kingdom of God is seldom visualised as a city, vibrant, energetic and filled with huge numbers of different nationalities: it is a small, human-sized community in which everyone knows everyone else, everyone is similar to everyone else, all have a place and all know their place.

EXERCISE

How do you envisage the Kingdom of God?

What might the Kingdom of God feel like?

Community exodus

Gibson Winter's book, *The Suburban Captivity of the Churches*, sets the task of the church against this mobile background. In his book, Gibson (1961, p. 18) observes the flow of suburban movement:

> The decentralisation of metropolitan population follows a distinct pattern: moving outward from the heart of the central city to the rural hinterland, one finds progressively more expensive housing, more education, and higher incomes; as one approaches the centre of the metropolis, the residents are increasingly unskilled, their incomes lower, their dwellings poorer.

While his analysis was done in America it clearly has some relevance to the United Kingdom. Suburbia is also for us a place on the way outwards. House prices rise as you move away from the city centre and the inner city. Racial homogeneity, as described by Winter, also increases as the population withdraws. The inner cities of many of our cities have far larger populations of ethnic minorities than suburbia.

This mobility is important to observe and to begin to understand. The place of a particular part of suburbia within this pattern affects many of the questions and issues that the church must face. In answering the question 'Where is suburbia?' we must first understand where it is coming from and where it is going.

Dissatisfaction and aspiration

If suburbia is not as static and stable as it appears, then neither is it as complacent as those outside it believe. Dissatisfaction is a crucial element in understanding the dynamics of its being. To answer the question 'What is suburbia?', it is essential to know something of the individual biographies of its inhabitants. Such questions are, of course, the raw material of social analysis. They function to discover the class, income, education, employment and status of those questioned. More importantly they seek to discover change in these areas; discovering the background and predicting the future of where the children will go – to which college, to what career; and asking where parents have come from and how present positions were obtained. Such stories, gathered together either informally in the course of pastoral care or formally as part of a church audit, will reveal something of the dissatisfactions and aspirations of the community.

These stories are often of effort and aspiration: from relatively humble backgrounds, through supportive parents, imaginative teachers, to colleges and further training; a move socially and educationally away from home that is both gratifying but dislocating. It is the story of a man who lived in the inner city, won a scholarship to a grammar school, whose parents and relatives contributed toward the costs of uniforms and compensated for lack of earnings: a man who now runs a large department of a college. It is the story of a woman who, while failing the eleven plus, succeeded in going to teacher training college and is now a head teacher. Such stories explain why apparently middle-class professionals are uneasy in their relationships with other professionals, and uncomfortable in the social settings of suburbia. The great prize is not all that was hoped for, and yet its winning has meant losing all the connections that previously were enjoyed. Like Hans Christian Andersen's mermaid, each step can be agony.

Such journeys are profoundly influential. They can determine many priorities and ambitions. The two fundamental elements, success and disjointedness, lead to the longing for stability and connectedness. Having lost a place in one community by the ambitions of that community, the need to discover a new place and a new community become essential. Who we are is not simply a matter of who we are in ourselves, but also in our relationships and society. Suburbia is the product of a movement towards stability that was created by instability. It is the dynamic of a sprinter who is unstable unless moving, and moves to keep balance.

The word dissatisfaction is not meant to imply a grumpy group of complaining people. It is a deeper sense of discomfort than that. It is the dissatisfaction that lies behind personal ambition and a social conscience. To look at where you are and long for things to be different is the motivation that drives one on to individual success and, at times, to attempt to alter the world for others. In his book *The Wound of Knowledge*, Rowan Williams (1979, pp. 75–76) provides the following reflection on St Augustine of Hippo's classic study *The City of God*:

> It was Cain who built the first city: it was the first murderous despiser of God who built an earthly home while Abel remained a 'pilgrim' ... To be in the way of salvation is to be dissatisfied, 'disquieted within', never complacent about your condition, or secure in your understanding or your stable spiritual attainment.

While it is not the case that suburbia is profoundly religious, the inherent discontent and longing for the new makes people open to the possibilities of a spiritual journey. Of course such a journey is not exactly the same as the suburban journey, and the conflict between these two reactions to the same need characterises something of the Christian agenda in suburbia. In such discontent and inner disquiet you find both the problem and hope. Here lies the field 'white unto harvest'.

EXERCISE

📖 **Read Hebrews 11:8–10.** The letter writer describes the faith Abraham demonstrates when he leaves home for the Promised Land. When Abraham hears God's call he is prepared to leave his familiar settled existence behind. But even when he arrives in the Promised Land Abraham still looks forward to the future city of God. ▶▶

> How might this passage from scripture speak to the church in sub-
> urbia?
>
> To what extent does suburbia stand as the 'promised land' in con-
> temporary society?
>
> To what extent should Christians endorse or challenge this?

Perception and reality

We have described the gulf that exists between the initial perception of
suburbia and the underlying reality. It exists in the appearance of
stability and calmness, covering the reality of change and movement.
It exists also in the appearance of contentment, covering unfulfilled
aspirations and discontent. This gulf is not an incidental observation to
the social analysis of suburbia. It is a central theme. Suburbia wants,
needs, demands to be misconstrued.

Peter Berger (1969) describes the efforts to which human beings go
to preserve the social reality they have created. If, as Berger claims, any
society is a human product, then it is inherently precarious and transitory, constantly liable to be undermined by human self-interest or
stupidity. One might add that suburban society is perhaps, by its very
nature, particularly precarious and transitory. As Gibson Winter (1961,
p. 75) puts it: 'The new middle class is a traditionless group. Its position
in the world is very uncertain.' Human beings construct social order to
preserve themselves from the horror of chaos and meaninglessness.
Berger argues that the fear of chaos and meaninglessness is a fear greater
than the fear of death, and human beings will go to great lengths to preserve themselves from it. Religion is particularly good, he adds, at 'legi-
timating' social order and lending it 'ultimate', all-embracing meaning.

> **EXERCISE**
> Do people actually fear chaos and meaninglessness more than
> death?
>
> Have churches been mistaken about people's actual concerns? ▶▶

Are people in suburbia likely to have a greater fear of change?

Has the church tended to legitimate the suburban status quo?

Suburbia appears calm because stability is an essential longing. The need to create the appearance, to hang on to the dream, is a fundamental suburban need. It is the reality that is longed for. That this stability is not obtained or even, arguably, obtainable, is an essential thing to know. For to fear change is inherent in such a place. A great deal is risked if change is introduced: conservatism of whatever political colour is the inevitable consequence. When considering change it is always a helpful idea to consider the risks that the different groups involved face. These risks will not be identical for all concerned. In management SWOT analysis has been popular. This asks what are the strengths, weaknesses, opportunities and threats that an organisation faces. The clear threat in suburbia is often change itself. While the longing for change is the motivating power behind suburbia, the change that is longed for is stability. This apparent paradox accounts for the almost obsessive need for normality and changelessness. Complacency, smugness and resistance to change do not flow out of confidence and self-satisfaction. Quite the reverse; like the earlier rule of thumb, they imply the opposite.

Suburbia appears content, even complacent, because contentment is also an essential longing. The appearance is maintained because the reality is needed and failure is unacceptable. It is the anger of poverty or fear of it that fuels the discontent, driving populations outwards from deprivation. To face up to the reality of discontent, while needing to preserve the reality of success and contentment, is thus a far more threatening and risky business than for someone who lives in the knowledge of the perceived inadequacy of their community. It may be too simple to put it this way but it makes the point. If you have striven all your life to live in suburbia, committed yourself financially for the next twenty years to pay to live in suburbia, you will find it difficult to accept the reality of the instability of suburbia and its inherent discontent. There is a dark and light side to such an observation. Clearly the striving, personal responsibility and longing generate energy that is both creative and helpful. The dark side is the destructiveness to happiness and relationships. In his disturbing book on the psychology of evil entitled *People of the Lie*, M Scott Peck (1983) looks at the damage that an inability to face up to failure can generate. The real danger of suburbia believing its own self-image is not the trivialisation that suburbia receives from the world in general, but that those people who live there become incapable of accepting the failure of the dream.

In the next chapter we shall be considering how the suburban church might be helped to reawaken from its failed dreams and to become more fully Christ's as it moves outwards.

Further reading

Fishman, R (1987), *Bourgeois Utopias: the rise and fall of suburbia*, New York, Basic Books.

Silverstone, R (1996), *Visions of Suburbia*, London, Routledge.

8. AWAKENING FROM THE FAILURE OF THE DREAM

Introduction

In this chapter we shall:
- continue to explore the particularities of the suburban context;
- compare and contrast the suburbanised church and the missionary church;
- outline a theological agenda for the suburban church.

Reflecting on experience
How important are boundaries in suburbia? How much attention is paid to erecting and maintaining fences, hedges and other boundary markers?

Is it true that in suburbia 'an Englishman's home is his castle'? Reflect on your own, or others', experience.

Disconnected and self-contained

Suburbia can be understood in its 'village' desire to be entire unto itself. Outside help is not sought, nor help to others offered. Here conservatism easily spills into Conservatism. The rejection of society as something that can be understood as something in itself motivates an individualist morality that has little room for social justice, the needs of the poor and the developing racial and social crisis of the inner cities. The local community in which I used to minister has gone further than most. We do not even choose local Conservative candidates but 'Rate Payer Association' candidates for the Local Authority. This group of independents proudly boast their complete indifference to the needs of anyone outside the local community. Unlike the local Conservative candidates, the only serious rivals, who display some obligations towards the nearby housing estates and some effort for social provision for the poor, the Rate Payers obtain a huge percentage of the local vote on the basis of exclusively local issues. Incidentally other more established suburban areas would find it easier to accept that, for some at least, poverty is not the result of lack of effort, dishonesty and profligacy. It must be underlined once again that suburbia is no *one* thing; 'Rate Payers' have far less hold in other areas which may instead be driven by a very strong sense of social conscience and belief in society.

In their recent report for the Joseph Rowntree Foundation, *Sustainable Renewal of Suburban Areas*, Gwilliam, Bourne, Swain and Prat (1998, p. 8) identified six types of British suburbs: the historic inner suburb, the planned suburb, the social housing suburb, the suburban town, the public transport suburb and the car suburb. Most suburban developments in Britain fit into either the category of public transport suburb or car suburb. The *public transport suburb* largely derived from the expansion of mass transit systems into the countryside in the first half of the twentieth century; the housing is usually homogenous, typically semi-detached, and of medium density; the social mix of each public transport suburb is usually quite limited: some are 'leafy suburbs' catering for the upper-middle classes, others are more ordinary suburbs for the working classes; individuals may move between different 'classes' of suburb during their lifetimes. The *car suburb* in the latter part of the twentieth century colonised some of the gaps not originally served by public transport and also the edges of the townscape; housing here is often lower density, again fairly homogenous, but typically detached; streets are wider and houses generally have garages. Inevitably, we are in this book mostly dealing with generalities but it is important for churches to discern the variations, as well as similarities, between different suburban contexts for ministry.

It is vital to recognise the gulf that exists between the initial perception of self-sufficiency and detachment, and the actual relationship of suburbia to the outside. For it is, of course, wholly dependent on outside for its inside prosperity, and largely motivated by elsewhere for its existing surface contentment. The mobility of suburbia as part of the exodus outwards means that its understanding of self must contain reference to where it is coming from and where it is going. The outside impinges upon its apparent stability. Each house becomes a fortress of lights, alarms and locks as the threat from less prosperous areas encroaches upon suburban castles. Images from television, more complex and challenging than soap operas, threaten the illusions that are so crucial to the maintenance of reality and effective defence against lawlessness.

Suburbia then, as we have seen in this and the previous chapter, is not a simple place but may be understood in a variety of ways, as:

- a place of social mobility, driven by hopes towards community and identity;
- a place of some discontent that longs for something better, both material and spiritual;
- a place of appearances, in which contentment, success, self-sufficiency and calmness belie a less acceptable reality;
- a place of apparent detachment that is actually inextricably bound up with where it has come from and where it wants to go.

Sustainability?

What future, if any, does the suburb have? Is the suburb sustainable long term? A recent analysis (Gwilliam, Bourne, Swain and Prat, 1998) has identified a number of the difficulties currently impacting some parts of suburbia:

- deteriorating housing stock, especially in older suburbs;
- lack of housing variety, and therefore an inability to cater for new housing needs in the context of family break-up and the rise of one-person households;
- declining local shopping centres and parades, offering a reduced range of shops and services, sometimes undermined by out-of-town retail development;
- deteriorating community facilities: leisure and health facilities, for instance, are often increasingly centralised elsewhere;
- a weakening sense of community;
- unsatisfactory and poorly integrated public transport provision;
- increasing car dependency, which not only increases congestion, energy consumption and pollution but also socially marginalises those who are not car owners;
- excessive land consumption, fuelling demand for more green-field building sites;
- visual monotony, reducing sense of local identity.

The analysis went on to suggest that the voluntary sector could play an important role in assisting the community process in suburbs at the local level, and increasing awareness of the difficulties facing suburbs at national level (Gwilliam, Bourne, Swain and Prat, 1998, p. 72).

EXERCISE

How might the church and individual Christians take up this challenge? Can you think of any other ways of addressing these issues? Might there be other issues for the church to address in suburbia?

The suburbanised church

Arguably the most influential study of suburbia by a theologian in the second half of the twentieth century was *The Suburban Captivity of the Churches* by Gibson Winter (1961), who was then teaching at Chicago Divinity School. Although a sympathetic critic of the suburban church, or 'organisation church' as he termed it, who recognised that most of its members had been 'drawn there by a deep search for the meaning of life' (Winter, 1961, p. 158), Winter lambasts the suburban church for its failure to be a vehicle of mission and ministry. He compares and contrasts the missionary church and the suburbanised church:

Missionary church	**Suburbanised church**
heterogeneous and interdependent	homogenous and insular
more universal community	identifies with local area
platform for mission	refuge for middle classes
agent for communication and reconciliation	shackled to local enclave
wide social base	identification with single class
proclamation and imaging of promise of reconciliation and renewal	affability and co-optation of those of similar social and economic background
community based on belief and worship	fellowship by likeness
representation of metropolitan community	substitute for metropolitan community
energies channelled into mission and ministry	frantic search for identity through 'vicious circle of activity'

church perceived as a means to an end	church perceived as an end in itself
extraverted church	introverted church
mission includes engagement with the public arena	mission restricted to arena of the family and leisure interests
experiences fullness of God's presence	experiences emptiness of middle-class life

According to Winter, the metropolis can only be properly understood in terms of two competing social factors: interdependence and insulation. On the one hand, the metropolis links together people of all kinds of backgrounds in a web of impersonal interdependence; on the other hand, the metropolis tends to divide into local residential neighbour-hoods, segregated from each other on the basis of class and ethnicity. The suburban church makes the mistake of identifying with a particular local residential neighbourhood and turning its back on the complex interdependencies of human life. The suburban congregation seeks to preserve its social homogeneity but how, Gibson Winter (1961, p. 29) asks, can the gospel's inclusive message be mediated through an exclusive group?

The suburban church becomes a middle-class refuge from the insecurities of rapid social change and urban decay, rather than a platform for Christian mission. The suburban church is tied to a local enclave which increasingly seeks to protect itself against outsiders. As Winter notes in one of his more recent books, *America in Search of its Soul*, suburbanites are now 'building walls of security around their homes' (Winter, 1996, p. 94). It is inner-urban, rather than suburban, churches that have learned the art of community building and have been agents of communication and reconciliation across class and racial divisions. Suburban churches are often very friendly and affable but their outreach is primarily through friendly contacts with people of similar social and economic position, which Winter terms 'co-optation'. By contrast, the outreach of missionary churches witnesses to the power of the gospel to transcend differences. Winter claims that suburban churches are first and foremost economic peer groups seeking fellowship with those of similar social background, and only secondarily are they believing and worshipping fellowships. The suburban congregation only represents a fragment of the total metropolitan community.

Much of its energy is channelled into its own organisation and activities, rather than into mission and ministry. Its members, in typically middle-class fashion, evaluate themselves in terms of what they can do and achieve, rather than how they feel or believe. This is a suburban version of 'salvation by works': 'a treadmill where men and women grind out their salvation' (Winter, 1996, p. 102). The missionary church sees itself as simply a means to a greater end; the suburban church is more interested in its own institutional survival than in mission. Whilst the missionary church is an extraverted church which intersects with the political, economic, social and cultural concerns of society, the suburban church reflects an introverted privatised gospel. The suburban church is preoccupied with the world of family and leisure, the problems of personal inwardness and emotional balance, the upbringing of children and preservation of neighbourhood harmony. In the process, religion tends to be sold short. The gospel is 'trivialised to an assurance that the emptiness of middle-class life is all that life was meant to be anyway' (Winter, 1996, p. 103).

EXERCISE
Look at the programme of a suburban church and compare it with the tasks in which Jesus engaged with his disciples.

Suburban churches had expanded, Winter claimed, at the expense of inner-urban churches. Denominations had disproportionately ploughed their personnel and resources into the suburbs. The solution, he suggested, lay in new forms of church organisation based not on the local parish but on 'sectors' carved out of the metropolis, like the wedges of a cake, which would include both the inner city and the suburbs. Only when churches were linked together in this way would ministry to inner-urban areas be properly resourced and the suburban church discover what it means to be a missionary church and to witness to the gospel of reconciliation.

Although much of Winter's analysis of American suburban churches is astute and transferable to the British milieu, his proposed 'sector' solution perhaps underestimates the ability of suburban churches to continue to call the tune. In practice, churches in the inner city have often found it more effective to develop alliances with other inner-urban churches.

The suburban agenda for the church

The suburban church, as any church, is called to preach and live the Kingdom of God. This is not simply a message of individual morality or social righteousness, but a call to reborn people in new relationships. The message of the Kingdom addresses directly the social context in which it is preached. The language of that message derives from that context. God's word thus engages in its own dynamic, in which what is said effects change among whom it is said and their society, and the society impinges upon the content of what is spoken. Moreover, that word is not spoken by an individual to society but through a community, the church. Words alone are not the carriers of the message, but the nature of the church itself proclaims its theme. The church is both message-carrier and part of the message. The church proclaims the good news of which it is also a representation. Another dynamic exists: the church itself drawn from the locality reflects that culture, and yet at the same time, drawn together by God's word, reflects that word. The process by which it engages in mission is a process of its own becoming.

In preaching and thus becoming the Kingdom, the church seeks to change at a fundamental level the dynamic that exists between it and the society in which it is placed. This task takes on a particular culture and direction when it is placed in suburbia. The questions that we ask are dependent on the social context in which we ask them. Furthermore, our ability to hear what is said depends on where we are placed. The word of God resonates with personality and context so that the same message is perceived and responded to differently according to by whom and where it is heard. Preaching the Kingdom and calling people to repentance – the essence of the gospel of Jesus – can neither be spoken nor heard without an understanding of the social context in which it is preached and listened to. The 'life situation' which provides so much valuable insight to the homiletic task also provides impetus to the task of social analysis.

What then must the church say in the suburban context? The key themes of Jesus' message both resonate with and disturb our churches. Preaching has been defined as the task of comforting the distressed and distressing the comfortable. Prophecy, existing in a wider field involving the whole church as a prophetic community, has a similar task. God's word resonates in the church to comfort or disturb. What comforts or disturbs depends on where people are in their journey. In this study we can only begin to outline the kind of theological work that needs to be done in the suburban context.

EXERCISE

What in the gospel message comforts you and what disturbs you?

The crucified God

The cross disturbs suburbia, as it should, and does so at a fundamental level. The importance of power, success, achievement – the force behind the dynamic of suburbia – is challenged head on by the God who is crucified. The extraordinary notion, stumbling block and folly that it is, becomes the key to all our theological understanding. In his book *The Crucified God*, Jürgen Moltmann (1974) explores the gulf that exists between our understanding of God and the God revealed on a cross. In a culture of self-sufficiency that longs for wholeness rather than holiness, that despises inadequacy and dependency, the notion of a crucified God who calls us to be 'wounded healers' is a disconcerting message (Nouwen, 1972).

EXERCISE

📖 **Read 2 Corinthians 12:9–10.**

How might this passage challenge conventional ways of thinking about what it means to be strong and weak?

The invisible poor

The detachment of suburbia (its self-sufficient independency and individualism) has a consequence in its attitude towards the poor. The gospel is clearly concerned for the poor and such a message naturally raises profound questions as to the mission priorities of the church. Luke records a story of Jesus that deals with this issue.

EXERCISE
📖 **Read Luke 16:19–31.**

With which character do you identify in this story? What might the story be saying to the rich and poor?

Martin Luther King Junior described this passage as a problem of invisibility, not one of wealth. The rich man suffers from an inability to see Lazarus at his gate. Luther King points out that Abraham, the example in the story of faith and righteousness, is also the richest man in the Bible. Gibson Winter observes the danger of such blindness to the long-term health of the church. He points out that Christianity has become the primary concern of the better off and educated on a number of previous occasions in history, most notably in China and in North African Christianity in the time of St Augustine. At that time the church all but died out leaving hardly a trace behind it. 'Where Christianity has become identified with upper-class élites, it has lacked a substantial base in the working population and has been unable to weather social change' (Winter, 1961, p. 49). The church, despite its urban funds and its constant preoccupation with the need to address the inner city and development issues, remains largely a suburban church. The poor remain in danger of being invisible to us, and this fact imperils the church.

This, of course, need not be the case. There is also evidence of the concern of the suburban church to see the poor and to react appropriately. Part of the comfort of this passage is to remind those who are disquieted that it is not a sin to be suburban. The sin is occasioned by an inability to allow the reality of disquiet and discontent to appear.

The London suburb of Clapham, some five miles from the City, was first developed in the late eighteenth century. One of the earliest examples of English middle-class suburbia, it was also home to many of the so-called 'Clapham Sect', an influential and prosperous group of Anglican evangelicals which included William Wilberforce and Hannah More. Although perhaps best known for their opposition to the slave trade, the Clapham Sect were also vigorous advocates of suburbia. They were convinced that Christian virtues were best fostered in the context of the family. Suburbs, they believed, were both family-centred and family-friendly; the overcrowded, unhealthy, vice-ridden city, on the other hand, undermined the family and its piety. Living in suburbia served to insulate their women and children from the city's baleful influences. But this did not necessarily mean that the Clapham Sect turned its back on its responsibilities to the wider world: it was in Clapham, for instance, that much of the anti-slavery campaign was planned.

Social change and stability

Suburbia resists change for good reasons, but does so at a time when surviving and managing change is essential for the church. It is clear why it seeks material prosperity, contentment and stability. Its inherent discontent and instability drive it outwards from the centre to a rural idyll. However, Jesus calls us in the other direction.

EXERCISE
📖 **Read Matthew 10:7–10.**

The disciples were told to travel light. Are these words meant to apply to followers of Jesus today? If so, how might you translate them into the contemporary context?

The call to insecurity and connection with those in need is to be spoken in the context of those longing for security and disconnectedness. The children of Israel discovered that manna had a short shelf-life: it could not be kept overnight. Such a story, among several others, indicates that our journey should be one in which we both travel light and learn to depend on each other and God. The exodus that creates suburbia is in a contrary spirit for it is moving away from dependency to self-sufficiency, from poverty to material wealth. Such a passage is both a comfort and a challenge. It offers a glimmer of hope to the materially trapped. It is a gracious invitation to be free. It is also disturbing for it demands a reassessment of what is considered safe and valuable.

The suburban dream and the Kingdom of God

The starkest contrast of aspiration and gospel message is focused in the theme of the Kingdom of God. Suburbia longs for a small community of similar people, self-sufficient, detached, where each person is known and knows their place. As Robert Fishman (1987, p. 154) has observed, the suburb can be seen as:

a testimony to bourgeois anxieties, to deeply buried fears that translate into a contempt or hatred for the 'others' who inhabit the city.

The Kingdom of God appears very different. It is essentially a city – a multi-cultural city in which all the nations gather. Here differences are taken up into one Lord, not filtered out by social mobility. Access to such a Kingdom is as children, not through the rise of the meritocracy. In this the poor will be lifted up, the rich sent away empty, and the sinner and the prostitute will have pride of place. The topsy-turvy nature of the Kingdom is not simply an irritant to the middle class, it is a fundamental criticism of their values. It challenges suburban values with Kingdom values and offers a new agenda for lifestyle and community. The rural dream that springs from disquiet is an unobtainable fantasy. Its pursuit leads to urban decay, to the gathering of the like-minded in more and more deeply entrenched ghettos. The gospel of the Kingdom, on the other hand, is one of hope that calls us back to the city we are leaving. This is not necessarily a geographical shift. It is rather a social one. It challenges perceptions of race, gender, poverty and class and invites the church to engage in a far more exciting and colourful future.

The eye of a needle

In first-century Palestine moral virtue was associated with material prosperity. The poor of the land were considered so because of their lack of holiness. The idea that the rich could in some way be disabled from a real understanding of God was thus a strange and new concept that Jesus brought.

EXERCISE

📖 **Read Matthew 19:16–24.** Here a rich young man asks Jesus how to obtain eternal life.

What do you think he expected Jesus to say to him? What might have surprised him about Jesus' reply?

This man is the archetypal suburban person! By striving, by a profound sense of personal discontent, by a developed conscience, he is driven to

Jesus. The message on the surface, to his surface appearance, is one of total despair. Here there is no comfort. The gospel resonates with an agonising discord. But the passage is not about the surface. It is not about the smooth suburban surface of success and stability: complacency. It is about the reality: the longing, the despair, the discontent, the commitment, the effort. The message is indeed one of hope of liberation. Jesus tells his disciples that the 'Kingdom is at hand' (Mark 1:15). It is there for the taking. In the context of all the discontent and longing, a message of hope is expressed in the beatitudes: to those who hunger and thirst, those who know their poverty, those who mourn and feel the pain – to all – a blessing. The key in all is to awaken to the reality of the dream and discover that theology is really all about grace, and ethics about gratitude.

EXERCISE

The gospel message resonates with the church in its context, disturbing and comforting. How do these themes in particular resonate with the suburban church? In what ways do they comfort? In what ways do they disturb? Consider the following challenges:

- Christ's love expressed by the **cross** – demanding dependency in the ethos of self-sufficiency?
- Christ's offer of **new life** – in the context of a community that longs to change?
- Christ's blessing of the **poor** – in a culture that makes poverty invisible?
- Christ's call to **follow** – in a place that wants to move, but seeks security?
- Christ's message of the Kingdom of **all nations** – to those who long for like-minded community?

The social analysis of suburbia reveals a particular theological agenda that addresses some of the underlying forces that occasion it. By discovering where people are coming from and hoping to go, the call to discipleship takes on a sharp and new focus. Wealth and privilege are not themselves the issues. The issue is the control such have on the community or the individual. How can the suburban church become the church of Christ? Suburbia revealed by social analysis has a different agenda from the gospel. This matters, for while the world's agenda must be taken seriously, the theological agenda of the gospel must also be allowed to play its part.

Further reading

Fishman, R (1987), *Bourgeois Utopias: the rise and fall of suburbia*, New York, Basic Books.

Silverstone, R (1996), *Visions of Suburbia*, London, Routledge.

9. VILLAGE PARADISE?

Introduction

In this chapter we shall:
- explore rural contexts for ministry;
- identify some of the consequences of increasing population movement into the countryside;
- analyse the nature of the 'village community'.

Reflecting on experience
What sort of things come into your mind when you hear the word 'rural'? Make two lists. In the first, list any positive associations; in the second, list any negative associations. Which list is more significant for you?

What is rural?

It is possible to see English society as comprised of a large middle section of urban and suburban areas with two peripheries. On one side is the inner city with its particular problems and needs and the awareness of rapid and accelerating change. On the other side are the rural areas where many believe that as yet the processes of change have had little impact. Twenty years ago conferences were held with such titles as 'The Dying Village', in which it was suggested that the impact of continuing depopulation in some remoter areas would lead to the gradual death of some rural communities.

The 1960s and 1970s saw what has been called 'a quiet revolution' in the countryside as a result of the impact of population migration and the subsequent 'embourgeoisiement' of village life. In a relatively short space of time depopulation was replaced by repopulation and the influence of the new villagers has profoundly altered the nature of many rural settlements. It was the recognition of the impact of a whole range of mutually reinforcing changes which prompted the Archbishops of Canterbury and York to appoint a Rural Commission, whose report *Faith in the Countryside* was published in 1990 (Archbishops' Commission on Rural Areas, 1990). The report echoes that of other rural organisations in drawing attention to the fact that the countryside is a separate arena in English society and should be understood as such. Whilst Americans tend to refer officially to their countryside as the 'non-metropolitan' areas, it is important to acknowledge that the countryside and rural villages have a specific history, culture and economy which needs to be acknowledged by those who seek to minister in such areas.

Generalisations about the countryside need to be approached with some caution; there are 44 different geological strata in Great Britain and, in traditional society, the underlying rock type was the principal determining factor in assessing local agriculture, architecture and settlement patterns. Today the dominant factor is proximity to the nearest urban area, and it is possible to identify four countrysides which are shaped like concentric rings around the nearest metropolitan centre: the urban shadow countryside; the accessible countryside; the less accessible countryside and the remote or marginal countryside.

The definition of what is rural in modern English society is both varied and complex. Some social geographers have developed indices of rurality, and planners and administrators have found it necessary to devise arbitrary delineations between urban and rural areas. However, the most commonly used definition of the rural population is that which regards it as those who live in market towns and villages of up to 10,000. There are approximately 13,000 such settlements in England and Wales, in which nearly twenty per cent of the population live. Of these settlements, 9,000 have a population of less than 1,000 and 80 per cent have a population of less than 500.

In the 1930s it became common to use the terms 'urban' and 'rural' not to denote location but to indicate different lifestyles. Commentators suggested that while the distinction between urban and rural areas was in many places difficult to maintain, nevertheless it was possible to speak of a rural culture which was significantly different from the dominant urban culture. However, it is increasingly difficult to see in what sense the distinction can be maintained in England in the last quarter of the twentieth century; everyone lives in an urban and industrial mass culture and people are exposed to the same media influences. Particularly in the younger age groups, all acknowledge the same cultural symbols, receive similar education, dress alike, watch television and share common or at least related aspirations and values. This is not to deny that there are attitudinal patterns, values, dispositions and modes of behaviour that are characteristic of those who live in the countryside (what the Americans call the 'rural mindset'). But it must be acknowledged that the degree to which the term rural can be used in this sense is problematic.

If it is difficult to define the term rural, it is equally difficult to define the word village. To the average English person the word village is like a telegram in code; at its mention the mind is flooded with a series of pictures, impressions and beliefs which have been reinforced in every generation by, among other things, the idealistic way in which the countryside and its people are treated in children's books. The village has become, in contemporary Britain, a symbol of that lost community and that lost sense of belonging that disappeared when society became more sophisticated and affluent. There is a real sense in which the village is a paradise from which the Englishman has been thrust out. Perhaps it is hardly surprising that one of the most industrialised and densely populated of countries should possess a deep sense of arcadianism and pastoral nostalgia. The dream of human innocence in the garden has deep roots. It is hard not to believe that some part of this nostalgia, this homelessness or rootlessness, is not itself part of a wider search for faith. Certainly for some, the countryside in modern Britain has become an object of faith and it is protected and venerated with what might be regarded as an almost religious intensity.

EXERCISE

📖 **Read Genesis 2:8–17.** Here a rural image is used to describe the original act of creation.

Try to imagine the Garden of Eden depicted here.

📖 **Read Revelation 21:1–4.** Here an urban image is used to describe the new heaven and the new earth. ▶▶

How accurate would it be to describe this as 'returning to paradise'?

Generalisations about villages tend to affront the belief that all villages are totally different, a difference which is both real and symbolic. Certainly, all villages have their own life, their own character and nature, much of it obscured and not easily accessible, and the church is often the custodian of the village's identity and its past. In a sense, a village is defined by its past, for a village is a community in time and the product of its history, which in part makes it what it is today. A consciousness of the past hangs heavily in many villages and there is a real sense in which the contemporary village is the product of its past. At another level it can be maintained that the people who move into villages today do so partly because they wish to be surrounded by the symbols of the past: the parish church, the village green, the black and white cottages, the old pub. Thus it is appropriate to preface any consideration of the contemporary countryside with a consideration of its past.

EXERCISE
How might the church function as custodian of the village's identity and its past?

Recent development of the village

Much that is written about the contemporary countryside is seen through the prism of the nineteenth-century rural community, and the 'golden afternoon' of the late Victorian and early Edwardian countryside has printed itself indelibly on the English imagination. Pictures of English rural history owe much to the artists and writers of the 1920s who had their imagination seared by Sanctuary Wood and Passchendaele Ridge and cherished such memories of the countryside as comforting symbols of the world that had vanished as a consequence of the First World War. However, in reality there was little that was romantic, picturesque or even 'golden' about the nineteenth-century countryside. Most of its inhabitants knew the harsh realities of rural poverty and the claustrophobic atmosphere of village life. Many of the clergy who moved from Oxford and Cambridge in the mid- and late nineteenth century for rural livings have left testimonies in their diaries to the deep sense of shock with which they encountered the squalor and misery of many of their parishioners and the brooding sense of violence and brutality, drunkenness and disease which dominated much of village life. The rural simplicity and community spirit which are described with such a wistful sense of loss by many of the books referred to, was in reality the brotherhood of hard work and poverty and the sisterhood of housekeeping in circumstances where hunger, dirt and disease were ever present. Blood, sweat and hunger are well known as strong social adhesives and much that is now called 'the loss of community spirit' in fact refers to the passing of these primitive conditions in rural England.

EXERCISE
Either read an autobiographical account of life in the countryside, such as Laurie Lee's (1959) *Cider with Rosie* or Flora Thompson's (1939) *Lark Rise to Candleford*, or visit a museum of country life.

How accurately is rural life presented here? What blindspots might there be? Did it make you feel nostalgic? If so, what generated that nostalgia? What might be the attractions and dangers of nostalgia?

Whilst in earlier periods the history of the village was determined by the history of the farming community, at least by the last quarter of the nineteenth century this was no longer the case. In the mid-nineteenth century, Surrey was a county of remote heathland and woods less valued for farming than many areas. The advent of suburban railways allowed the relatively wealthy the option of living in the countryside and commuting to town. The term 'commuting' is derived from the commuted rate at which railway tickets for regular journeys were issued. The period after the Second World War saw the development of garden suburbs and an accelerating increase in commuting from those villages within easy reach of metropolitan centres. The widespread availability of private cars and the surge of speculative building in villages, coupled with government action in the 1970s to encourage decentralisation, had a marked impact on many rural areas. Whilst the population of London in this period fell by approximately one per cent per annum, the attractiveness of living in the countryside caused the rural population in accessible rural areas to rise significantly.

Planning legislation dates from the mid-1930s when public opinion was alerted by campaigners such as Professor Joad to the dangers of uncontrolled sporadic ribbon development. In the 1940s the Town and Country Planning Act (1947) established a planning system based on the preparation of country development plans which provided the specific framework for planning for the next twenty years and the more generalised framework thereafter. The effect of this and much subsequent legislation has been to control development in rural areas, which has had the effect of raising the price of housing in the village.

It became increasingly apparent in the post-war period that it was not possible to provide facilities in every single community. Increasingly facilities were concentrated on key or capital villages, and central place theory (originally developed in America and Germany) has come to dominate rural planning in this country. Services and facilities have been provided in certain larger villages which serve a surrounding rural hinterland. In the smaller villages, almost no facilities are now available and this makes it increasingly difficult for those on low incomes to live in these communities. Conversely, the countryside has become more attractive as a place of residence and retirement, particularly since the 1970s when it has been perceived that the quality of life has been declining in urban areas. A recent survey has indicated that twelve million people desire to move to the countryside in the next ten years, and whilst this desire may not be realised in every instance, nevertheless the pressure of urban decentralisation continues to be one of the principal agents of change in the contemporary countryside. According to 1998 government estimates, at least 4.4 million new homes will be required in Britain by 2016; up to 2 million houses may need to be built on green-field sites.

Finally, no account of the contemporary countryside can be complete without acknowledging the role of the environmental movement in recent years. Whilst in an earlier period the countryside was seen largely in functional terms, today it is seen by many people as a place of recreation and as the habitat of increasingly endangered wildlife. Interest in these concerns has increased dramatically in recent years and was reflected very considerably in increases in membership in relevant organisations during the 1970s and 1980s (the membership of the Royal Society for the Protection of Birds increased from 6,803 in 1972 to 385,364 in 1984; the Caravan Club increased from 84,000 in 1970 to

250,000 in 1984). For many people the countryside is no longer seen principally as a place where people live and work, but as a recreational area and as a habitat for wildlife. This, as will be shown below, is already having a significant impact on many parts of rural Britain and the confrontation between concerns for the environment and concerns for economic development is one of the principal debates concerning the present countryside.

EXERCISE
Consideration of life in rural situations raises a number of environmental issues and dilemmas. On the one hand, there is the desire to preserve the countryside from the environmental effects of road transport; but on the other hand, rural dwellers are particularly dependent upon the car. Or similarly, we may not want to see more of the countryside taken over for major road developments, but nor do those living in villages want constant through traffic. Visitors to villages help the local economy (and provide custom for cafes, accommodation, craft shops, petrol stations), but they also pollute the environment. In Cumbria, and in some other areas, there is a conflict between the hazards associated with nuclear power and the need for jobs. What sort of balance should be established between these competing interests?

Whilst, in the early period, the village can be seen as an occupational community in which all were involved either directly in farming or in one of the ancillary or support trades, today the village is a more mixed community no longer centrally concerned with farming. Thus, the contemporary village can no longer be described as a single community focused around the demands of the farming year, but is more accurately described as 'a community of communities', comprised of the *farming community*, the *old village community* and the *new village community*. It is the interaction between these groups and their different perception of the nature and function of rural settlements that is of principal importance in any description of rural areas in England today.

The farming community

Britain's entry into the European Common Market in 1973 was the most important date in the post-war history of farming. Since then agriculture has taken place in an increasingly European context and today the principal decisions about farming are taken at that level. The effects of change within the farming community in the last generation have been to concentrate the farming of the English countryside in the hands of relatively few people. Today there are 281,000 farmers and it is estimated by some that approximately twenty farmers a day are leaving the land. However, farm production is concentrated in the hands of very few people. Approximately 30,000 farmers account for 60 per cent of production and it is estimated that, by the end of the century, twenty per cent of farmers will be producing over 80 per cent of agricultural output. A single family farming enterprise in Norfolk farms 9,000 acres, grows 15 million lettuces, 60 million carrots and produces 25 per cent of the UK parsnip crop, in addition to 3,000 acres of cereals and 1,700 ewes. Almost all the vegetable processing and packing takes place on the farm and large articulated lorries carry the produce to Tesco and Sainsbury's stores throughout the country. The whole operation employs between 900 and 1,100 people.

Scientific and technical advances, coupled with the economies of scale on larger farms, have led to a steady rise in agricultural production, and the problem of British farming has become the problem of over-supply. In essence, the need to control over-supply has become the dominant factor in contemporary British agriculture and two principal methods have been advocated. The first method has been an attempt to control the quantities harvested by direct intervention. Supply-control has been most successful in dairying, where milk quotas were first imposed on 30th March 1984. Although production declined initially by nine per cent, all existing milk farmers retain some stake in the market and quotas (the right to produce milk) became a saleable commodity. Quotas have also been introduced for potatoes and sugar beet. The other principal mechanism of supply-control is the fallowing of arable land known as 'set aside'. In recent years farmers have been encouraged to set aside fifteen per cent or more of their land in return for a fixed payment. There remains some doubt about the effectiveness of this (both in terms of cost and agricultural production) and the American experience indicates that volumes produced continue to rise as farmers set aside their least productive land and farm their better land more intensively. Farmers are now being encouraged to set aside areas of land on a more permanent basis either for forestry or for bio-mass production. The other principal means of control is that of price regulation. It is argued by many that price regulation is less effective as it does not of itself lower the total volumes produced and tends to concentrate production in the hands of the more efficient producers.

The determination of European governments to curtail spending on agriculture has led to a sharp decline in commodity prices, particularly in the arable sector, where some prices have fallen by nearly 40 per cent in two years. In the livestock sector, similar declines have been recorded as a result of BSE and changing dietary patterns as people move away from the consumption of red meat. The National Union of Farmers has demonstrated that in the last two years there has been approximately a 50 per cent decline in the profitability of English farms, which is likely to be followed by a further 36 per cent decline next year. A recent forecast by the National Westminster Bank indicated that 25,000 farmers (of a total of 170,000) are running businesses which are technically insolvent.

Historically, there has been a divide between an emphasis on arable farming in the eastern counties and livestock farming in the west. While this persists there has been a marked contraction in the number of people engaged in farming and a consequent increase in the size of units. Farming itself is a highly diverse activity ranging from large-scale, low-intensity livestock enterprises (such as sheep farming) to arable farming with different crop mixes, to intensive livestock (particularly poultry and pigs) and vegetable farming. In recent years in all sectors there has been a movement towards spreading production costs over larger acreages or larger numbers of livestock. At the same time scientific advances, especially the recent impact of genetic engineering and changes in management techniques, have also increased productivity and profitability.

However, in the contemporary farming scene there is a marked difference between the policies advocated by large-scale and by small-scale farmers. In previous decades, as can be seen above, a whole range of social and environmental payments have become available to farmers, which have had the combined effect of producing desirable environmental and social ends and of supporting farm incomes and thus retaining farm families on the land. Large-scale farmers want agriculture to become a strictly commercial enterprise from which all social and economic payments have been eliminated. If these are needed, these should be paid under a separate head. Such large-scale farmers, who are principally arable farmers in the eastern counties of this country, and in the Paris basin and Northern Germany, are agreed that they can survive only by spreading their fixed costs over a larger acreage and by selling their products on the world market. The contraction of farming has been such that an increasing number of farmers come into this category and it is paradoxical that land prices continue to rise during the recent recession as farmers attempt to operate over larger acreages.

By contrast, small-scale farmers believe that quotas and set aside and other comparable measures offer them better protection than a move to a 'level playing field' situation which could have the effect of squeezing them out of the system. Many small farmers appreciate that it will not be possible for them to derive their total income in the future simply from the sale of agricultural commodities. They realise that some of their income will have to come from social and environmental payments, that is to say government and European grants made to farmers for environmental enhancement schemes, access to the countryside or simply to retain the presence of the farming community in remote areas, often for tourist reasons (as in central France, the Austrian Alps and the English upland areas). Other small-scale farmers see their future in diversification, and 40 per cent of the farmers in the south-west derive significant income from a variety of non-agricultural on-farm sources, many of them related to the holiday and leisure industries. The third category of small-scale farmers see their future in part-time farming, where the farmer (or a member of the family) derives a significant part of their income from a job off the farm (as in Bavaria).

Farmers acknowledge that their present situation is politically vulnerable as it is unlikely that the larger sums currently paid to the farming community can be maintained in the future. Farming represents 3.4 per cent of the European Community's GDP but 66 per cent of its budget is spent in agricultural support. One farmer recently received over a million pounds for set aside and other payments, and clearly such high levels are unlikely to be sustained in the future. Storage costs of the surplus of 36 million tons of wheat and 1 million tons of beef mean that every British family is paying £530 per annum in direct support for the farming community.

In recent years there has been a significant increase in the influence of environmental groups, including animal welfare organisations.

Farmers, who once were seen as the saviours of the nation, providing essential foodstuffs, particularly during time of war, have increasingly been cast in the role of the spoilers of the countryside and the enemies of its wildlife. Thus, farmers see themselves more and more as an isolated group, misunderstood and frequently attacked by the wider society. The village in which they once played a leading role has become increasingly populated by those who do not understand their way of life and are disposed to attack certain aspects of it. A farmer in evidence to the Archbishops' Commission said that farming and food production was a subject of constant local criticism and abuse, leaving his family feeling strangers in the church in which they and their ancestors had worshipped since 1650. Whilst even as late as the inter-war period the agricultural community was the dominant element in the rural population, it is now a small and beleaguered part often exposed to the hostility of new rural residents and increasingly turned in upon itself. The growing incidence of stress and suicide within the farming community has led to a campaign to alert farmers to these issues in recent years.

EXERCISE

📖 **Read Psalm 8.** The second half of the psalm speaks of the dominion that humanity has been given over the natural world. This has sometimes been interpreted in terms of domination and exploitation, but is more accurately interpreted as careful stewardship or caretaking.

📖 **Read this Celtic Christian prayer:**
Bless, O God, my little cow,
Bless, O God, my desire;
Bless Thou my partnership
And the milking of my hands, O God.

Celtic Christians experienced the nearness of God in creation. Their prayer grew out of the daily rhythms of life, including such an apparently mundane event as milking the cow. To what extent does your practice of spirituality encourage you to be more responsible and gentle towards creation?

Further reading

Archbishops' Commission on Rural Areas (1990), *Faith in the Countryside*, Worthing, Churchman.

Blythe, R (1951), *Akenfield: portrait of an English village*, London, Allen Lane.

Bowden, A (1994), *Ministry in the Countryside*, London, Mowbray.

Davies, D, Watkins, C and Winter, M (1991), *Church and Religion in Rural England*, Edinburgh, T and T Clark.

Francis, L J (1985), *Rural Anglicanism*, London, Collins.

Francis, L J (1996), *Church Watch: Christianity in the countryside*, London, SPCK.

Lewis, R and Talbot-Ponsonby, A (eds) (1997), *The People, the Land and the Church*, Hereford, Diocesan Board of Finance.

Newby, H (1985), *Green and Pleasant Land? social change in rural England*, Harmondsworth, Penguin.

Newby, H (1988), *Country Life*, London, Cardinal.

Phillips, D and Williams, A (1984), *Rural Britain: a social geography*, Oxford, Blackwell.

Rural Development Commission (1991), *English Village Services in the Eighties*, London, RDC.

Rural Development Commission (1992), *Homelessness in Rural Areas*, London, RDC.

Rural Development Commission (1993), *Rural Transport Problems and Needs*, London, RDC.

Rural Development Commission (1993), *English Rural Communities*, London, RDC.

Rural Development Commission (1994), *Lifestyles in Rural England*, London, RDC.

Russell, A (1980), *The Clerical Profession*, London, SPCK.

Russell, A (1986), *The Country Parish*, London, SPCK.

Russell, A (1993), *The Country Parson*, London, SPCK.

Van de Weyer, R (1993), *The Country Church*, London, Darton, Longman and Todd.

Williams, R (1985), *The Country and the City*, London, Hogarth Press.

10. COUNTRYSIDE CONTRASTS

Introduction

In this chapter we shall:
- explore rural contexts for ministry;
- analyse the countryside as a place of social contrasts;
- examine the role of the church in the rural community.

Reflecting on experience

What is your 'central point of stability' – your career or your house in a local community?

How often have you moved house? Have you moved far?

Which group do you identify more closely with, the new or old villagers?

The old village community

In the popular imagination, villages are seen as inhabited by those whose forebears have lived there for a number of generations. However, in most villages today only a few families have a long connection with the village. One of the most distinctive features of the modern village is the division between 'the new villagers' (commuters, retired people and weekenders) and the old village community, those who live in the village and work, if not in the village at least in the area. The old village community are the inheritors of the traditional understandings about village life which go back to the time when the village was almost exclusively an occupational community.

The different attitudes between these groups can be noted at many points, but particularly with regard to employment and housing. The new villagers, who are predominantly middle-income earners, tend to be centrally concerned with the development of a career line; for them the central point of stability is their job and they will change houses and districts according to the progress of their career. They are the 'colour supplement gypsies' whose roots do not lie in a physical but in an occupational community. By contrast, for the old villagers, who are predominantly lower-income earners, it is the house in the local community which provides the point of stability. For them, once they have found a house (whether rented, owned or tied) they tend to remain in the same house but change jobs according to local employment opportunities. Thus it is common to find men who once worked on a farm, and then in the construction industry, lorry driving or with the local highways department. For the old villagers the centre of their life is the home and the local community to which they are tied by membership of the local social network and in many instances by extensive kinship linkages. Put briefly, the lives of the new villagers are defined by their job and the old villagers are defined by kinship and place. Clearly, this divide is becoming increasingly blurred in the contemporary village, but it is still important analytically in trying to understand the dynamics of contemporary rural communities.

The old village community, impoverished by those who have moved away but enriched by its struggle to retain its own identity, echoes at many points the pre-industrial understandings and values of the village. Kinship is of particular importance, and even where the old village community now forms a relatively small part of the total village, the kinship map, complicated by generations of cousin marriages, is still an important part of the reality of the village. This knowledge is often used by the old village community as a means of maintaining their distinctiveness and of excluding the more recently arrived residents. The old village community, even when it is reduced to just a few families, often retains a sense of being an alternative and hidden community with its own leadership, its own occasions and places of significance. Sometimes the church, the parish council or the British Legion hut remains the preserve of the old village community, who have in a sense retreated into a stronghold from which they can preserve something of their identity.

The economy of the countryside, on which many of the local population depend for employment, is diverse, in some areas under five per cent of the jobs relating to farming and its ancillary trades. The rural economy is characterised in certain areas by dependence on certain major employers, which leaves it particularly vulnerable when these job opportunities are lost. The impact of the peace dividend is having a major effect in certain areas, as are changes in the mining, quarrying and extractive industries. The incidence of home-work is particularly striking, with approximately one fifth of all rural workers working from their homes. Approximately 30 per cent of all rural workers are self-employed. These figures together indicate a relatively high level of small home-based businesses in rural areas. However, these and other businesses often find difficulties in expanding, owing to the dominant view that the countryside is not an appropriate place for such activities.

In contemporary society, people have come to regard deprivation as an urban neighbourhood phenomenon. The overall impression of the countryside as a place of affluence often disguises the existence of a considerable degree of deprivation which, unlike urban areas, is scattered over a large area, rather than concentrated in particular neighbourhoods. However, the incidence of deprivation in rural areas is both high in overall terms and spread throughout the community. In the countryside, deprivation tends to be hidden, dispersed, unorganised and frequently relatively inarticulate. The government has recently announced a Rural White Paper which comes in the wake of the move towards Regional Development Agencies and the setting up of the Countryside Agency (merging the Countryside Commission and the Rural Development Commission). Among a number of factors it is recognised that levels of social exclusion and poverty in rural areas are higher than is generally supposed. The feeling that rural areas and rural communities have been neglected, which has led to the centralisation of facilities and services and the closure of village schools, has been recognised in the government's intention to develop a rural component to regional policy.

It is one of the paradoxes of social change in the contemporary countryside that the new villagers who have brought affluence to many rural communities and have restored cottages that were once in an advanced state of decay, have also contributed to the cycle of decline in services and facilities in rural areas. Many of those people make almost no demands on local shops; the possession of a car (or two cars) allows them almost exclusively to use urban and suburban services. For these and other reasons, there has been a decline in all rural services in recent years and many villages have lost either their school, shop, post office or doctor's surgery or, in some cases, all of these services. Such retail services as remain in certain rural areas are now provided by petrol stations, as in the United States. For the approximately 30 per cent of households without a car, and for members of households who do not have regular use of the family car, the consequences of poor public transport, in terms of reduced opportunity for work and training, and access to essential services and social services, can be severe.

In many rural areas low family income provides an additional problem when the costs of transport and other facilities are often higher than in urban areas. For instance a car, which might be regarded as an inessential item in an urban area, can hardly be seen as such in the countryside where without transport a household's opportunities for work and their access to services and facilities are severely restricted. However, recent research has shown that in many rural areas twenty per cent of households are classified as being in or on the margins of poverty; the numbers are particularly high in rural Nottinghamshire (39 per cent) and Devon (34 per cent). The problems of rural living are exacerbated for vulnerable groups, especially the elderly, the unemployed, women (especially lone parents with children), the disabled and young people. One of the major concerns of the modern rural community is to develop effective mechanisms for measuring, and suitable indicators for demonstrating, the extent of rural deprivation.

However, no issue has dominated the countryside in recent years so much as that of rural housing and particularly the lack of affordable housing for those on relatively low incomes. This concern pre-dates the 'right to buy' legislation of the 1970s which allowed residents to purchase their council houses and thus effectively withdraw them from the village housing stock. As this happened at the same time as rural house prices were rising steeply as a result of increasing demand from urban dwellers to move into rural areas, housing in the village passed well beyond the level at which it could be afforded by local residents. A recent report has indicated that homelessness (as officially defined) has continued to rise, particularly in the more remote areas where it has risen at the fastest rate, but it has also risen significantly in the rural south of England. In 1992/1993 11.6 per cent of the national homeless total were in rural areas. However, homelessness in the countryside, like other aspects of deprivation, tends to be hidden and many near-homeless families are living in temporary accommodation (often used for holiday-makers during the summer). In 1993 (excluding London) twenty per cent of the national total of those in temporary accommodation were in rural areas. The Rural Development Commission study of 1992 concluded that there was a net requirement in rural areas of 80,000 additional homes. There is a heavy reliance on housing associations to build in the countryside and this work has been pioneered by the Rural Housing Trust. Whilst as a result of the work done by housing associations the situation has improved, the fact remains that an increasing number of the old village families find that their children have to move out of the village as they cannot afford accommodation in rural areas.

EXERCISE

📖 **Read Micah 4:1–5.** Here the prophet looks to a time of universal peace, when God will be rightly obeyed and worshipped. Everyone will live secure in their own home 'among (their) own vineyards and fig trees' (v. 4). Note that when the prophet envisages the salvation that is to come he speaks of people finding rest and security in their own physical homes, as well as finding their true spiritual home (vv. 1–2).

📖 **Read Deuteronomy 24:19–22.** In these laws, designed for an agrarian community, the needs of the poor, powerless and marginalised are addressed. Because the Israelites have themselves, in their collective history, experienced what it is like to be exploited and to be redeemed, they are expected to act compassionately towards those in the rural community who fall by the wayside.

What are the implications of these passages for today?

The new villagers

Whilst in the nineteenth century some people were disposed to regard the village as in some ways similar to an open prison from which those who could made their escape to the city, by contrast in the twentieth century an increasing number of people wish to make the journey in the opposite direction. As a result, many villages have lost almost all vestige of the days when they were an occupational community, and have become mixed residential settlements. The proportion of old and new villagers varies considerably in different parts of the country, but in most areas a process of population substitution has been taking place during the decades of this century by which a variety of new villagers have taken the place of those who once lived and worked in the countryside.

The work of rural sociologists in the Second World War and immediate post-war period, such as the study of north-west Oxfordshire villages by C S Orwin (1944) and his team, was principally concerned to bring home to a wider public the degree of social disintegration which has affected the majority of villages. Such studies make pessimistic reading and they cannot be blamed for failing to anticipate the wave of migration to the countryside, as depopulation gave way to repopulation in the second part of the twentieth century. The widespread availability of private transport, the extension of the public transport network and the improvement of the rural infrastructure encouraged many to move to rural areas and contributed to the transformation of the demographic structure in most European countries and in the United States. By the 1970s demographers were aware that a significant population shift was taking place and many urban areas, which had recorded steady population growth for many decades, were now declining.

Whilst those who move to the countryside do so at any age, nevertheless it is possible to suggest that two groups predominate. The first group is those with young families who have recently outgrown their urban and suburban first homes and seek to bring up their children in the country. Many of the new families arriving in the villages in the more accessible countryside are those with young children, whose main breadwinner has a managerial or professional job, who move into a new house on a private development on the edge of the village or who purchase and restore one of the cottages (possibly two converted into one) in the centre of the village. The other group, who typically form a large proportion of the new households in the village, are those who have either reached retirement age or are anticipating retirement in the foreseeable future; many people move to the countryside in their mid-fifties and early sixties (what the Americans call 'the empty nest move'). It is well known that the period of bringing up young children and that of retirement are both times in the life cycle when people have to adapt to new circumstances, stresses and constraints. Indeed, there is a degree of complementariness between the two groups, for under the dispositions of traditional society it is the grandparents who play a major role in the life of young children. It is possible to suggest that among the many and varied reasons for making these moves, people in these two groups are, consciously or unconsciously, influenced by the view of the village as a warm, accepting community which in some way acts as a surrogate extended family, in an age when the psychological need for the extended family is still evident but such families are often scattered across the countryside. Those who move into the village form three groups: those who commute, the retired, and occasional residents (those with second or holiday homes).

EXERCISE

Do people tend to see the village as a warm, accepting community which acts as a surrogate extended family? How far is the village likely to measure up to these hopes?

Commuting now affects almost all of lowland England and despite the high cost both in money and in time, it is the preferred lifestyle of many people. Dr Johnson expressed the opinion that heaven would contain the joys of the countryside and the amenities of the town, and many are seeking to achieve this compromise. Those who choose to live in the countryside and commute to an urban job are seeking a quality of life for their home and family which they believe does not exist in the city and are willing to make considerable financial sacrifices and to endure the problems and costs of long-distance commuting. They value being a part of a small-scale historic community and being surrounded by the comforting symbols of the past. At the same time, many place a high value on self-reliance, independence and privacy which they believe to be more congruent with a rural rather than an urban life. The garden is the symbol of many of these values and the 'home-centred culture' is a marked feature of the commuter's lifestyle. Behind this lies the more fundamental desire of modern individuals to separate out the various compartments of their life and particularly to distance their work life from their family life. The effect of commuting has been to turn many villages into discontinuous suburbs, from which the men are absent during the working day. The women and children often find themselves stranded without a car in a remote village and some of the contemporary social problems associated with rural communities are in consequence of this.

If commuters are the typical new residents in the urban shadow villages, then amongst those who move to the more accessible villages the retired predominate. Retirement migration is the most significant current demographic factor in English society. Between 1971 and 1991 it is estimated that the number of retired people in rural areas has increased at double the rate of urban areas. Retired people are often particularly vigilant in seeking to protect and retain the village in what they believe to be an appropriate circumstance and are often among the first to resist planning applications either for new houses or for change of use. Many retired people often find that there are fewer facilities and services in rural areas than they imagined and many find that, within ten to fifteen years of having moved to a relatively remote village, they need to move again to a larger village with more adequate services. The second retirement move is now becoming a relatively common phenomenon and appropriate accommodation is being built in many of the larger villages and market towns. Second home owners are present in some numbers in almost all parts of the countryside, though in significant numbers they tend to be clustered in particularly desirable or scenic areas. There are now some villages in the Lake District and in north Devon where all the houses are owned by those who do not live there throughout the year. The increasing view of the countryside as a place of recreation has brought to rural areas a migrant population, some of whom live in caravans and purpose-built holiday accommodation but others have bought houses in the village. In many areas this is resented by the overwhelming majority of the rural population, though some derive from it new sources of employment and income.

The word community is often applied to villages which are seen from the outside as harmonious, integrated settlements. It can be seen from the above that the population of the modern village is mixed and is drawn from a number of different groups. The relations between these different groups are not always harmonious, as they do not have the same ideas about what the village should look like, smell like and feel like as a community in which to live. Many of those recently arrived in the village are surprised by the high level of conflict which is often apparent in many rural communities. Whilst it is not easy to generalise, and there are many rural settlements to which this may not apply, nonetheless there is often evidence of some degree of tension between the farming community and the rest of the village; between the old resident community and those who have recently arrived; between those who think that the countryside should be a place of work and those who regard it principally as a place of residence, recreation and retirement. What happens in any particular village is the consequence of the interaction between these different groups. Behind all the more pressing and acute problems concerning employment, settlement patterns, transport, land use, housing, education, social and welfare provision, changing agricultural practices, conservation, landscape and heritage protection, and more general questions about the future of the village, lie these different models and understandings of what the rural community should be. The farmers see it as the shop floor of Britain's largest industry; the old village community see the village as their home, the place where they need facilities and services to sustain an acceptable lifestyle; commuters and the retired see the countryside as a place of residence and retirement; and finally second home owners and occasional residents and the non-resident urban population see the countryside predominantly as a place of recreation and refuge away from the pressure and stresses of modern urban living.

Changing roles for the rural church

In order to minister in such a situation churches need an appreciation of the background to modern rural settlements and some understanding of the way they have developed. At the same time they need to be multi-lingual so that they can relate to the different groups who are present in the rural community. The church has an ancient and acknowledged place in almost every village; it is regarded as the repository of the village's history as well as of the family history of many of the older village families.

EXERCISE

📖 **Read Hebrews 13:7–8 and Deuteronomy 6:20–25.** Each passage attaches importance to remembering the past. Because God is consistent, God's action in the present and future will be in harmony with God's action in the past. Understanding God's action in the past will shed light on God's action and the Christian pilgrimage today (Hebrews 13:7).

📖 **Read Isaiah 43:18–19 and Mark 2:22.** There is some tension between these passages and the others. The prophet (known as Second Isaiah) highlights the danger of dwelling in the past. God is identified as the God of new things, a God who ▶▶

beckons us into a future which may explode our presuppositions, much as new wine bursts an old wineskin (Mark 2:22).

Should the church uncritically accept its role as custodian of the
village's identity and its past?

How might the church best be an agent and herald of God's Kingdom?

Though regular week-by-week attendance has fallen in many rural
areas, the results of the work of the Rural Church Project demonstrated
that attendance at special services within the village remains high
(Christmas over 50 per cent, Easter and Harvest approximately 40 per
cent); that 75 per cent of the village were likely to have been to at least
one service during the course of the year; and that 30 per cent of the village were likely to have attended at least once a month. Unlike urban
areas, the church does not have to fight its way in; it has an acknowledged part in the rural community and though it is easy to dismiss some
of this as 'mere folk religion' it does still present the church with considerable pastoral opportunities and responsibilities.

EXERCISE
Folk religion has been described as 'quasi-religious beliefs and
practices' and as 'unorganized, inconsistent, heterogeneous and
changeable' (McGuire, 1987, pp. 89–90).

Is 'folk religion' the opposite of 'true religion'? Or might it be seen
in terms of the first tentative steps by human beings responding to
their Maker?

On the eve of the First World War there were approximately twice the
number of Anglican clergy than there are today and a much higher proportion of them ministered in rural areas. The church came close to
having a clergyman in almost every rural settlement and almost all
aspects of church life were organised directly by the clergyman and his
family. As a consequence, church life in England became highly depen-

dent upon the clergyman and attitudes of deference and dependence have persisted. In many communities there remains a 'parson-shaped hole', and still in the eyes of some the clergy are expected to run the church for the benefit of the local community.

Since the end of the First World War there has been a steady decline in the number of Anglican clergy in rural areas. Today, many clergy find themselves ministering to clusters of parishes and as a consequence their role has changed. No longer are they able to run the church in an old-fashioned way but they are required to lead, resource and invigorate a team of people who together share in the work of ministry. This team will in many areas include non-stipendiary and locally ordained ministers as well as Readers and lay people commissioned to certain tasks.

EXERCISE

Is your church run in an 'old-fashioned' autocratic way or is it run by a collaborative ministry team? If you have had experience of both approaches, which has been the most fruitful?

What might God be saying to us through the changes that have been occurring (for pragmatic and other reasons) to rural clergy roles?

Though the number of clergy has declined, the number of churches that have been closed have been relatively few and rural communities will still raise very large sums of money in order to safeguard the future of their church building. The future of the church and the countryside lies in the development of appropriate-sized pastoral units and in the development of ministry teams who can share in the work of ministry within a cluster of parishes. In many places the new people who have arrived in the village have brought new life, enthusiasm and ideas to the rural church which continues to witness to the gospel within the village, but in very changed circumstances.

Further reading

Archbishops' Commission on Rural Areas (1990), *Faith in the Countryside*, Worthing, Churchman.

Blythe, R (1951), *Akenfield: portrait of an English village*, London, Allen Lane.

Bowden, A (1994), *Ministry in the Countryside*, London, Mowbray.

Davies, D, Watkins, C and Winter, M (1991), *Church and Religion in Rural England*, Edinburgh, T and T Clark.

Francis, L J (1985), *Rural Anglicanism*, London, Collins.

Francis, L J (1996), *Church Watch: Christianity in the countryside*, London, SPCK.

Lewis, R and Talbot-Ponsonby, A (eds) (1997), *The People, the Land and the Church*, Hereford, Diocesan Board of Finance.

Newby, H (1985), *Green and Pleasant Land? social change in rural England*, Harmondsworth, Penguin.

Newby, H (1988), *Country Life*, London, Cardinal.

Phillips, D and Williams, A (1984), *Rural Britain: a social geography*, Oxford, Blackwell.

Rural Development Commission (1991), *English Village Services in the Eighties*, London, RDC.

Rural Development Commission (1992), *Homelessness in Rural Areas*, London, RDC.

Rural Development Commission (1993), *Rural Transport Problems and Needs*, London, RDC.

Rural Development Commission (1993), *English Rural Communities*, London, RDC.

Rural Development Commission (1994), *Lifestyles in Rural England*, London, RDC.

Russell, A (1980), *The Clerical Profession*, London, SPCK.

Russell, A (1986), *The Country Parish*, London, SPCK.

Russell, A (1993), *The Country Parson*, London, SPCK.

Van de Weyer, R (1993), *The Country Church*, London, Darton, Longman and Todd.

Williams, R (1985), *The Country and the City*, London, Hogarth Press.

REFERENCES

Archbishops' Commission on Rural Areas (1990), *Faith in the Countryside*, Worthing, Churchman.

Archbishop of Canterbury's Commission on Urban Priority Areas (1985), *Faith in the City: a call for action by church and nation*, London, Church House Publishing.

Barnes, R P (1991), Ecumenism and the whole (Christian) world, *Christian Century*, 108, pp. 390–392.

Berger, P (1969), *The Social Reality of Religion*, London, Faber and Faber.

Borland, J, Fevre, R and Denny, D (1992), Nationalism and community in North West Wales, *Sociological Review*, 1, pp. 49–72.

Citizen Organising Foundation (1997), *Reweaving the Fabric of UK Society*, London, Citizen Organising Foundation.

Clark, D (1973), Membership and intercommunion, in J Kent and R Murray (eds), *Community, Membership and the Church*, London, Darton, Longman and Todd.

Cox, H (1965), *The Secular City*, London, SCM.

Crow, G and Allan, G (1994), *Community Life: an introduction to local social relations*, London, Harvester Wheatsheaf.

Dale, J and Foster, P (1986), *Feminists and State Welfare*, London, Routledge and Kegan Paul.

Dennis, N (1968), The popularity of the neighbourhood community idea, in R E Pahl (ed.), *Readings in Urban Society*, Oxford, Pergamon.

Etzioni, A (1995), *The Spirit of Community*, London, Fontana.

Fishman, R (1987), *Bourgeois Utopias: the rise and fall of suburbia*, New York, Basic Books.

Frankenberg, R (1969), *Communities in Britain: social life in town and country*, Harmondsworth, Penguin.

Gill, R (1992), *Moral Communities*, Exeter, Exeter University Press.

Gladstone, D (ed.) (1995), *Thomas Chalmers 1780–1847: works on economics and social welfare*, London, Routledge.

Gwilliam, M, Bourne, C, Swain, C and Prat, A (1998), *Sustainable Renewal of Suburban Areas*, York, Joseph Rowntree Foundation.

Hammond, J and Hammond B (1995), *The Labourer*, Gloucester, Alan Sutton.

Küng, H and Kuschel, K (1993), *A Global Ethic: the declaration of the Parliament of the World's Religions*, London, SCM.

Kureishi, H (1990), *The Buddha of Suburbia*, London, Faber and Faber.

Lawless, P (1989), *Britain's Inner Cities*, London, Paul Chapman.

Lee, L (1959), *Cider with Rosie*, London, Hogarth Press.

Leech, K (1988), *Struggle in Babylon*, London, Sheldon Press.

Lewis, O (1959), *Five Families*, New York, Basic Books.

Lewis, O (1961), *The Children of Sanchez*, London, Secker and Warburg.

Lewis, O (1964), *Pedro Martinez*, London, Secker and Warburg.

Lewis, O (1965), *La Vida*, New York, Random House.

Lewis, O (1968), *A Study of Slum Culture: backgrounds for La Vida*, New York, Random House.

Linthicum, R (1992), Authentic strategies for urban ministry, in R S Greenway (ed.), *Discipling the City*, Grand Rapids, Michigan, Baker Book House.

Mawson, A (1995), Ten key elements of community regeneration, in E Blakebrough (ed.), *Church for the City*, London, Darton, Longman and Todd.

Mawson, A (1995), Community regeneration, in E Blakebrough (ed.), *Church for the City*, London, Darton, Longman and Todd.

Mayer, P (1961), *Townsmen or Tribesmen*, Cape Town, Oxford University Press.

McGuire, M B (1987), *Religion: the social context*, Belmont, California, Wadsworth.

Moltmann, J (1974), *The Crucified God*, London, SCM.

Morisy, A (1997), *Beyond the Good Samaritan*, London, Mowbray.

Mumford, L (1996), What is a city?, in R J LeGates and F Stout (eds), *The City Reader*, London, Routledge.

Newham Monitoring Project (1991), *Newham: the forging of a black community*, London, Newham Monitoring Project/Campaign Against Racism and Fascism.

Nouwen, H J M (1972), *The Wounded Healer*, Garden City, New York, Doubleday.

Orwin, C S (1944), *Country Planning*, Oxford, Oxford University Press.

Peck, M S (1983), *People of the Lie*, New York, Simon and Schuster.

Recinos, H J (1992), *Jesus Weeps: global encounters on our doorstep*, Nashville, Tennessee, Abingdon Press.

Richter, P and Francis, L J (1998), *Gone but not Forgotten: church leaving and returning*, London, Darton, Longman and Todd.

Rushdie, S (1988), *The Satanic Verses*, London, Viking.

Russell, H (1995), *Poverty Close to Home*, London, Mowbray.

The Methodist Church and NCH Action for Children (1987), *The Cities*, London, NCH Action for Children.

Thompson, F (1939), *Lark Rise to Candleford*, Oxford, Oxford University Press.

Tönnies, F (1957), *Community and Society: Gemeinschaft und Gesellschaft*, East Lansing, Michigan, Michigan State University Press.

Williams, R (1979), *The Wound of Knowledge*, London, Darton, Longman and Todd.

Wink, W (1992), *Engaging the Powers: discernment and resistence in a world of domination*, Minneapolis, Minnesota, Fortress Press.

Winter, G (1961), *The Suburban Captivity of the Churches*, New York, Doubleday.

Winter, G (1996), *America in Search of its Soul*, Harrisburg, Pennsylvania, More-house.

Young, M and Willmott, P (1957), *Family and Kinship in East London*, London, Routledge and Kegan Paul.

Applying for the Church Colleges'
Certificate Programme

The certificate programme is available in Anglican Church Colleges of Higher Education throughout England and Wales. There are currently hundreds of students on this programme, many with no previous experience of study of this kind. There are no entry requirements. Some people choose to take Certificate courses for their own interest and personal growth, others take these courses as part of their training for ministry in the church. Some go on to complete the optional assignments and, after the successful completion of three courses, gain the Certificate. Courses available through the *Exploring Faith: theology for life* series are ideal for establishing ability and potential for studying theology and biblical studies at degree level, and they provide credit onto degree programmes.

For further details of the Church Colleges' Certificate programme, related to this series, please contact the person responsible for Adult Education in your local diocese or one of the colleges at the addresses provided:

The Administrator of Part-time Programmes, Department of Theology and Religious Studies, Chester College, Parkgate Road, CHESTER, CH1 4BJ ☎ 01244 375444

The Registry, Roehampton Institute, Froebel College, Roehampton Lane, LONDON, SW15 5PJ ☎ 0181 392 3087

The Registry, Canterbury Christ Church University College, North Holmes Road, CANTERBURY, CT1 1QU ☎ 01227 767700

The Registry, College of St Mark and St John, Derriford Road, PLY-MOUTH, PL6 8BH ☎ 01752 636892

The Registry, Trinity College, CARMARTHEN, Carmarthenshire, SA31 3EP ☎ 01267 676804 (direct)

Church Colleges' Programme, The Registry, King Alfred's College, Sparkford Road, WINCHESTER, SO22 4NR ☎ 01962 841515

Part-time Programmes, The Registry, College of St Martin, Bowerham Road, LANCASTER, LA1 3JD ☎ 01524 384529